Analysing
Allerzielen Alom

Sidestone Press

MASTER THESIS COMPARATIVE RELIGION
INSTITUTE FOR RELIGIOUS STUDIES
FACULTY OF HUMANITIES
LEIDEN UNIVERSITY

Analysing Allerzielen Alom

Material Culture in an Emerging Rite

William R. Arfman

Supervisors:
Prof. dr. A.F. de Jong (Leiden University)
Dr. Thomas Quartier (Radboud University Nijmegen)

© 2011 by William R. Arfman

Published by Sidestone Press
  www.sidestone.nl
  Sidestone registration number: SSP29430002

ISBN: 978-90-8890-061-7

Cover design: Karsten Wentink, Sidestone Press
Cover photograph: Oski Collado 2007 and Peter van Lieshout 2009

Layout: William R. Arfman

Contents

Preface		7
Introduction		9
Chapter One: Theoretical Considerations		11
1.1	Implicit Religion	11
1.2	Ritual Dynamics	15
1.3	Material Culture	19
1.4	Theoretical Tools	22
Chapter Two: Introducing Allerzielen Alom		25
2.1	Allerzielen Allicht and Herinnering Verlicht	26
2.2	Allerzielen Alom	29
2.3	A Website and a Booklet	34
2.4	The Survey	36
2.5	Discussion	38
Chapter Three: Visiting Allerzielen Alom		41
3.1	Herinnering Verlicht in Amsterdam	42
3.2	Allerzielen Alom in Alphen aan den Rijn	45
3.3	Allerzielen Alom in Groningen	48
3.4	Allerzielen Alom in Apeldoorn	51
3.5	Allerzielen Alom in Castricum	54
3.6	Discussion and Analysis	57
Chapter Four: Developing Allerzielen Alom		61
4.1	Alphen aan den Rijn: Maintaining the Initiative	61
4.2	Apeldoorn: Local Adaptation	63
4.3	Castricum: Community Celebration	65
4.4	De Nieuwe Ooster: Dealing with Success	67
4.5	Ida van der Lee: Embedding the Concept	68
4.6	Discussion and Analysis	70
Conclusion		73
References		75

Preface

My personal academic interest in the intersection of material culture, ritual action and the dead was sparked in the town of Mitla in southern Mexico. Here I came across a dilapidated chapel standing on an eroded pre-colonial pyramid, where indigenous people of the entire region came to make traditional offerings to their ancestors and ask them for favours. The next year I came back for fieldwork, which resulted in an M.Phil. thesis about the cultural continuity behind this practice. When I decided to continue my academic development by following an M.A. in comparative religion I decided to look for a research topic in The Netherlands that would similarly involve objects and rites, and would allow for a combination of theoretical research and fieldwork. While visiting the Ritual Dynamics Conference in Heidelberg in October 2008, I also attended one lecture by Dr. Thomas Quartier, member of the 'Refiguring Death Rites' research group from the Radboud University in Nijmegen, and one by dr. Erik de Maaker, former member of that same group. Both dealt with a new form of celebrating All Souls' Day, and since the topic not only fitted in perfectly with what I was looking for, but was also related to my previous research in Mexico, my interest was immediately piqued. Talking to them later, I learned that that De Maaker had had to abandon his research on the phenomenon and that although the research group was still working on it, they did not mind me looking into it as well.

Thus having decided to pick this topic for my thesis, I had to quickly decide which of the celebrations to visit, and come into contact with their organisers. For their immediate, and ongoing, cooperation I would like to thank Ida van der Lee, Carla van der Elst, Hedi Hegeman, Anneke Pier, Alinde Vrolijk, Marina van der Wal and Raldi Beentjes. For their academic advice and support I would like to express my gratitude to my supervisor prof. De Jong of the Leiden University as well as dr. Thomas Quartier for advice and access to his previous research on the topic. Finally, I would like to thank my sister Annemiek, my mother Leida and my father Gerrit for their support, and of course my girlfriend Corinna, without whom none of this would have been possible.

Introduction

After sunset, on the fifth of November 2008, around 1200 people visited the Onderlangs municipal cemetery in the Dutch town of Castricum. The cemetery itself was brightly light up by torches standing besides its footpaths, candles and lanterns burning on most of its graves and some artificial light illuminating the main points of congregation. Most of the visitors to the cemetery were busy with such things as elaborately decorating the graves of their beloved ones, sharing some food and drinks with family, friends or other visitors, writing messages to those that they had lost on slips of paper to hang them in a young potted tree, listen to a woman playing a Tibetan singing bowl, writing the name of their dearly departed on a small paper flag so it could serve as an indication of the flower bulb just buried, or even with walking between a couple of doors over which a poem about leaving was distributed. Judging from their conversations, they were having a good time, even though difficult topics, such as loss and grief, were not being shunned. An uninformed passer-by might very well have wondered what exactly it was that was going on there that evening. Was it an art project? A religious ritual? A community celebration?

The evening in question was an Allerzielen Alom[1] celebration and it was far from the only such celebration, as there were nine others celebrated all over the country at roughly the same time. For 2009, sixteen are already being planned, which, given the fact that the first related celebration was organised by the Dutch artist Ida van der Lee in 2005, shows that the phenomenon is a rapidly spreading one. Combined with the fact that at Amsterdam's De Nieuwe Ooster cemetery and memorial park, where that first celebration was organised, approximately five thousand people visited in 2008, it becomes clear that, apparently, there is an underlying societal 'demand' for these events.

From an academic standpoint, this seems relevant as well. Because, independently of how exactly one would categorise the evenings in question, it will be evident that what goes on is relevant to our understanding of the processes of secularisation and individualisation, which supposedly dominate our society. Another opportunity presented by this case stems from the fact that material

---

[1] Allerzielen Alom: Dutch for 'All Souls' All Around'.

culture, whether an artistic installation of poetic doors or a strip of paper addressed to one's dearly departed, plays an important role during these celebrations. And it is precisely our understanding of this role that is, academically speaking, underdeveloped when it comes to the study of emerging ritual-like phenomena like Allerzielen Alom, and their relation to the above mentioned societal processes. To make a small contribution to the increase of our understanding pertaining to this role, the question investigated in this thesis will therefore be: Does material culture influence the present development of the Allerzielen Alom celebrations? And if yes, in what way and to which degree?

To come to an answer to these questions, chapter two will first introduce the background of the Allerzielen Alom project by describing its development up until the 2008 celebrations as well as previously conducted research. Next, in chapter three, a more in-depth description and analysis of the 2008 celebrations will be given, with a special focus on the position of material culture. This will then be followed up in chapter four, where the ways in which the organisers of the 2009 celebrations relate to material culture during development, will be studied. Finally, in the conclusion, the results of these three chapters will be summarised and discussed to come to an answer to the questions posed as well as to formulate relevant follow-up questions that could guide future research. Interestingly this structure, by being of a diachronical nature, also roughly follows the development of the underlying research as chapter two reflects initial reading, whereas chapter two is based on the ethnographic fieldwork conducted during the 2008 celebrations in Amsterdam, Alphen, Apeldoorn, Castricum and Groningen, while chapter four is the result of interviews with the organisers of these same celebrations concerning their plans for 2009.

However, before chapter two will introduce the Allerzielen Alom case, we will first have a look at some theoretical considerations pertaining to what is called implicit religion as well as at some key concepts from the fields of ritual studies and material culture studies. The object of these considerations is to formulate some theoretical tools, or heuristic devices, with which the matter at hand can be analysed in a manner going beyond mere description. In doing so, this study could also be seen as a test of the applicability and usefulness of these concepts for the study of material culture in emerging ritual-like phenomena.

Chapter One:

Theoretical Considerations

At the beginning of the introduction a question was posed regarding the nature of the Allerzielen Alom events described there. This chapter will seek to address that issue by considering the potential utility of the fairly recent concept of implicit religion, coming forth from the sociology of religion. Next, the related subject of ritual dynamics will be considered, with a special focus on the coming into being and subsequent development of new rituals. Finally, the basic concepts of material culture studies will be introduced, as far as they are relevant for this particular case. In particular, this means a focus on object-person relationality. Finally, on the basis of a summary of these three considerations, the conceptual tools mentioned in the introduction will be formulated in the concluding section.

1.1 Implicit Religion

The concept 'implicit religion' originates from the 1997 work of Edward Bailey entitled 'Implicit Religion in Contemporary Society'. In it, Bailey asks himself the question what form religious experience takes in the secularised present day Western world (Bailey 1997:3-4). The first reaction to such a question of course would be that secularisation precludes the existence of religion in any shape or form. Bailey however argues that such an idea of antagonism between being secular and being religious could only be kept up if religion were to be defined as *"an organised institution or a self-conscious ideology"* (Ibid:5). For although modern day people might not self-consciously identify themselves with organised religious institutions, and could therefore be called secular, this does not mean that they cannot also consider themselves religious in a less clearly defined sense, since such disjunctions are in practice rarely resolved, but largely ignored instead (Ibid.). These underlying, unresolved, non-organised religious feelings he then called implicit religion, which is not so much an antonym to explicit religion, but that which explicit religion institutionalises (Ibid:7-8; 42; 48). Bailey defines implicit religion either rather vaguely as 'commitment' or somewhat more elaboratively as 'intensive concerns with extensive effects' as well as 'integrating foci'. The latter is especially interesting as it further develops the idea of implicitness, by showing that through being implicit the divisions used to categorise human experience are integrated in such a way that they are prevented from becoming the kind of dichotomies that hamper a more holistic understanding of these experiences (Ibid:7-8). All three definitions are however fuzzy enough to become the target of the kind of accusations often brought against post-modern ideas, namely that with these concepts anything can become religious as such designations are highly subjective. To such accusations, Bailey answers firstly that in theory indeed anything could indeed be religious, as there are no a priori limits. This does not however mean that anything also is (equally) religious, as the distinction between religion and non-religion is more usefully seen as a continuum. Secondly, he points out that subjectivity is an unavoidable, even essential, aspect of understanding in the humanities and the trick is to interpret phenomena without also, positively or negatively, evaluating them (Ibid:45-6). The point of studying implicit religion therefore is not to preconceive of what should or should not be studied but to take the complete range of human experiences and then ask the question: *"What are the foci of personal life in this situation?"* (Ibid:49). And only by doing this, can the field of religious studies free itself of its historically biased focus on explicit belief by showing that it is *"empirically possible [...] to be thank-full, without* necessarily *thanking any personalised one or any personalised thing"* or *"to pray, without formulating any concept of a being to whom one prays"* (Ibid:47).

Talking about non-institutional religion, Meerten ter Borg in his acceptance speech for the Chair in Non-institutional Religion in Modern Society at the University of Leiden, pointed out that this concept is only of use if it is founded upon a theory of human beings as inherently religious (Ter Borg 2008:127). His proposition therefore is that religion is the consequence of mankind's ability to transcend the limits of the here and now, by imagining other possible worlds, whether heaven and hell or 5-year business plans (Ibid:128). Imagination here works as a two-edged sword: on the one hand people are able to ponder their finitude to the point of total despair, on the other hand this same imagination can create entities that limit the impact of these negative worldly forces, compensate them, or give purpose to it all. These entities can be anything ranging from gods, to spirits, to abstract principles such as Beauty (Ibid:129). Religion then functions to provide ways to overcome despair and restore ontological security. Thus, when the latter is threatened, the intensity of religion will increase (Ibid:130). Imagination however is not enough, as the imagined worlds and entities also need to have credibility in order to have effect. Such credibility can be generated in two ways, according to Ter Borg, either through the pressure of the ontologically threatening occurrence or through the self-reifying effect of tradition (Ibid: 130-1). If such credibility is explained on the basis of something not merely transcending the individual but this world altogether, it can be called explicit religion, and when it is less deliberately based on the things of this world, it can be called implicit religion (Ibid:130). Non-institutional religion and implicit religion are therefore not by definition the same thing, although just as Bailey does for implicit and explicit religion, Ter Borg argues that institutional religion comes out of non-institutional religion, when people start agreeing about the way in which things should be done.[2] He however adds that the relation between the two is dynamic as non-institutional religion exists side by side with, and can come forth of institutional religion (Ibid:132-3). The latter seems to be going on in the western world at the moment, and according to Ter Borg this is because secularisation made religion appear harmless again, while at the same time the new scientific worldview became unhinged. To this could also be added the process of globalisation and the end of the clear structures provided by the Cold War (Ibid:133-136). In its development, these new non-institutional forms of being religious are characteristic of contemporary western culture, with its extreme individualism, mass society, commercialisation, and the need for continuous innovation (Ibid:137). As such the people interested in these forms of religion are looking on a religious market for the sacralisation of the self, in new, non-traditional, ways amongst the masses instead of tied to a community (Ibid:136-9). As such it is *"mostly fragmentary and ad hoc, and is on permanent standby for any occasion when ontological insecurity comes under threat"* (Ibid:136). Ter Borg admits that such a model of religion is abstract and purely functional, pertaining merely to religion's use as a survival mechanism, and thus doing no justice to any existing

---

[2] Note that due to Ter Borg's distinction between non-institutional and implicit religion, this does not by definition entail that the religious phenomenon in question would also become explicit religion, as such an institutionalisation could be effected without conscious otherworldly justifications.

religions. He however also maintains that such an approach is justified because of what it can explain (Ibid:131). Problematically his approach seems to be based on the acceptance of the actual existence of something called religion, which can then take various forms, and Ter Borg could therefore be accused of being rather essentialist. In following Jonathan Z. Smith, it might therefore be worthwhile to point out that the concept of religion is first and foremost developed *by* religious studies scholars *for* religious studies scholars (Smith 2004:179-96). Thus, the question if religion really exists, is indeed of a much lesser relevance than the question if something can usefully be studied with this particular model of religion, a point very similar to the one made by Bailey.

Going back to the relation between ontological insecurity and the need for religion, it is interesting to see that Catherine Bell in her seminal work on ritual studies, entitled 'Ritual: Perspectives and Dimensions' states that ritual-like behaviour "*seems to reassure people that they can release their grief in a safe and ordered context that will not allow them drown* (sic) *in horror and helplessness*" (Bell 1997:240). Such a statement might lead one to wonder whether such behaviour could be another way of gaining credibility, as Ter Borg calls it. Bell herself seems to think so, as she states that the more ritual such behaviour becomes, the more natural it will seem, because then people tend to see themselves as responding, not creating (Ibid:167-8). This is partially due to the use of traditionalism[3] in such settings (Ibid:168), but another important reason that people locate the forces forming such occasions outside of their own influence (Ibid:169), is because these types of activities "*do not particularly encourage a great deal of immediate and overt explaining*" (Ibid:167). There is an 'effective ambiguity' (Ibid:232), that frames the action in such a way that it conveys an 'extra significance' (Ibid:166). Underlining the same societal processes as Bailey and Ter Borg, and coming to the same conclusion regarding religion (Ibid:199-202), Bell explains that the effect these processes have on present ways of thinking about what can be done with ritual, have effectively created a new model for it[4] (Ibid 171-2). In this model, ritual is less bound by any specific tradition but is instead a medium for psychosocial change, it is directed inward instead of outward and defines the community in relation to the self, instead of the other way around. As a result,

---

[3] More on this subject can be found in the next section.
[4] Here Bell argues that a change in the academic understanding of the concept can be seen as the foundation for this change in how western society sees ritual (Bell 1997: 162-3; 165).

ritual must be judged to be effective, or at least affective, as there is no longer any tradition to reify it (Ibid:240-1). In other words, instead of the idea that secularisation and individualism would mean the end of traditional ritual life, there now is a 'championing of ritual', where ritual will save humanity from the dehumanising effect of these same processes (Ibid:258). Consequentially, instead of basing their authority on tradition, these new ritual forms, at least implicitly, base such authority on the perceived universal importance of ritual itself (Ibid:263-4). Ritual, because of its effective ambiguity, thus seems to be, or have become, a crucial way in which imagination can be become more credible, so as to confront ontological security.

1.2 Ritual Dynamics

With the position of ritual in relation to implicit religion already having been stressed above, it would be worthwhile to delve somewhat deeper into that topic. It would however not be of much use if it would not mimic some of the fluency inherent in the concept of implicit religion. A straight forward, a priori, definition that would clearly demarcate ritual from other behaviour would therefore not do. Luckily, it is precisely this view that is put forward by Bell when she argues that ritual is best seen as a quality of acting, which is present to a lesser or greater degree in any instance (Bell 1997:138,164). Consequentially, she synthesised a list of six characteristics of ritual-*like* activities: formalism, traditionalism, invariance, rule-governance, sacral symbolism and performance (Ibid:138-164). This list will serve here as inspiration for the discussion of four aspects of ritual actions[5]. Hereto the first four categories are contracted into one, recursivity, while a fourth aspect, ritual as communicative, is added on the basis of the work of Roy Rappaport (Rappaport 1999). To stay away from any claims of ritual's essence, the terms are primarily used in adjective/adverbial form: so not ritual as being performance, but ritual as performative. Additionally, this opens up the possibility to qualify the degree to which a specific act is more or less performative. Finally, in addition to being described as aspects of ritual, they can also be used as angles, i.e. as means of looking at ritual from four different perspectives.

The first, and also the most agreed upon, of these angles is recursivity, or the idea that what is being done is seen as relating

---

[5] For a lengthier discussion of these four aspects, see Arfman 2008.

back to similar past acts. Although related to the concept of repetition, there is an important difference between it and recursion, because whereas repetition means that a past act is simply repeated again and again, recursion merely indicates that the current act is related back to one or more past acts, which may or may not lead to repetition in the strict sense. In other words, recursion means that what is done in ritual is never seen as a completely new and one-time act. It is something that is viewed as extending the past into the present. Here it is important to stress the word 'viewed'. A rite does not actually have to have a long past, it must only be interpreted as such. Thus, a rite must at least seem to be a repetition of something very much like it to be accepted. It must be seen as the natural way of doing things, not some strange new invention. As already mentioned in the previous section, it is from this feeling of great time-depth that a big part of a rite's credibility or effectiveness stems, it makes it seem older, and thus more authentic and enduring, than the immediate situation, which also makes it less contestable. The four characteristics listed by Bell could simply be seen as ways to either enforce recursivity, through rule-governance or otherwise maintaining invariance, or invoke it, through acting more formally or traditionally. Although it was posited above that new forms of ritual behaviour are much less often reified through such recursive mechanics, Bell also points out that ritual-like activities can be seen as mimicking an older model within a very short time span. Because with the mere addition of such statements as 'of our ancestors' or by showing how to do things 'like older people do it' the assumption that this was always done in such a way easily slips in (Ibid:150; 252).

The second important aspect of ritual behaviour is that it is symbolic, both on a cultural and on an individual level. The cultural symbolism of ritual action stems from the fact that rites are mostly not personal on the spot inventions, as already discussed above, and therefore have symbolically encoded within them a culture's categories. Because of this symbolic aspect, ritual behaviour can make things that are fairly unsubstantial such as spiritual, supernatural or higher beings into something concretely present, and therefore much easier to understand. Besides these cultural meanings, ritual can also be symbolic on an individual level. Due to difference in e.g. upbringing, personal experience and personal interest, different individuals will often subscribe different or even contradictory personal meanings to a ritual act. In this way it can become a palimpsest of various and possibly contradicting cultural and individual meanings. This mostly, however, will not threaten its function, because even though different participants may come into a ritual setting with different expectations, it can evoke these personal and collective feelings in a non-explicit way, without actually going into any underlying conflicts (Ibid:158).

A third aspect of ritual acts is its performative nature. In every account of every ritual from all over the world there is one thing that will certainly bind them: something is done. Ritual acts are not merely ideas or concepts, they involve actual activity. As such, they have a multi-sensory quality to them, so that, instead of something merely being told, it is instead experienced with the entire body (Ibid:160). For a great part this is the consequence of the way in which ritual action is framed in such a way that a specific setting is created, a temporary ritual world, that distinguishes this action from other actions. While the participants mostly feel that they are only responding to this framed setting, in actuality it is their own embodied actions that constitute it and give shape to it (Ibid:81-2; 139; 156-7; 168). It is largely because of the implicitness of this 'experiencing while constituting', that the messages communicated in this ritual setting gain such credibility as they do.

Coming thus to the fourth and least discussed aspect, ritual as communicative, an important question would be: What kinds of messages are being communicated in these ritual settings? An interesting view regarding that question comes from Roy Rappaport who argues that there are roughly two types of messages being transmitted: canonical and self-referential (Rappaport 1999:51). Canonical messages inform us about ever-lasting truths that transcend the here and now, while self-referential messages inform us on the *current* physical, psychic or social state of a group or an individual (Ibid:51-5). Of course these two streams of messages are in practice far from mutually exclusive. Specifically, it is through the type of framing discussed above that they are brought together in a symbolic and recursive setting. In that way not only credibility is gained, but is closely tied in with the current state of affairs of those participating.

When going beyond the characteristic aspects of ritual into the topic of ritual dynamics, we are presented with a problem when it comes to the implicitness that has been stressed several times so far. Because if ritual owes its credibility or effectiveness to its ambiguity than it can at best be gradually layered and re-layered, not explicitly and consciously changed, let alone be invented (Bell 1997:210-1). Such a conclusion would however go against actual practice, where ritualists are constantly carefully planning, observing and critically analysing ritual actions (Ibid:223; 225) To get a clearer sense of such practices, Ronald Grimes, one of the founders of ritual studies, attempted to clean up the terminology used to denote ritual behaviour (Grimes 2000:28). To do so he made a distinction between ritual, being the broad category, rites, being specific culturally recognised ritual acts, and ritualisations, being acts that are not so defined but could be interpreted as somehow related, akin to what Bell calls ritual-like behaviour. Ritualisations can become rites when their ritual qualities increase in such a way that they become culturally recognised (Ibid). When this increasing is done in a deliberate manner, Grimes speaks of ritualising (Ibid:29). Using the four aspects discussed above it could thus be said that the more performative, communicative, recursive or symbolic behaviour becomes, the more it is ritualised and the more one deliberately makes behaviour performative, communicative, recursive or symbolical, the more one is ritualising it. It is this latter activity then that is often seen as counter to the implicit nature of rites, because it deals too explicitly with imagination and invention (Ibid). Of these two, Grimes considers invention to be the more important one when ritualising, because if imagination is not given shape through invention, then it is of no effect (Ibid:4). It could be said however that different ways of imagining lie at the basis of the two models that Grimes distinguishes for the invention of new ways of ritualising, namely the somewhat inelegantly titled plumber's model and the diviner's model (Ibid:12-13). Because whereas the plumber encounters an issue and imagines creative ways of solving it, the diviner waits until the imagination brings up new ideas of its own accord. In other words, whereas the former is more of a hands-on, practical way of being inventive, the latter is a more circumspect and artistic way of being creative. Mostly, different groups of people will follow different models, although without *"both maintenance and mystery, the celebration cannot go on"* (Ibid:13). Given the constant involvement of these people it should be clear that *"[r]ites are not givens"* (Ibid:12), they do not *"spring into being full-blown and healthy. Some die in their infancy, some in adolescence. A few make it to old age and become venerable. Others, regrettably, hang on well beyond their years"* (Ibid:51). When studying the development of a ritualisation or rite, it might be worthwhile to extend the above analogy by speaking of its biography. In such a biography attention could be paid to the various features that were either taken from a rite and added to other rites, as well as those that were taken from other rites and added to this rite, so that it would be placed in a network of relations. This idea of transfer has been most thoroughly elaborated by the Ritual Dynamics research group of the University of Heidelberg (Langer e.a. 2006: 1-10). On the basis of their studies of the transfer of whole ritual systems as well as singles rites, they created a tool to analyse this form of ritual dynamics that consists of a matrix with a list of a rite's contextual aspects on one side and a list of its internal aspects on the other. The theory being, that if a rite is transferred, i.e. one of its contextual aspects is changed, then one or more of its internal dimension will also change (Ibid:1-2). As already mentioned above, it is not only rites themselves that can be transferred, but also specific features of them, such as certain actions, utterances or objects. In that case, the new rite itself is the contextual aspect that has changed (Ibid:3). Using the four aspects discussed above, this means that when such things as a rite's location, history or surrounding culture change, it will also become performative, communicative, symbolic and recursive in a different way. Therefore ritualising can not only result from increasing these internal aspects, but also from people deliberately changing its contextual aspects in way that has such an increase as a consequence. This importance of the people involved in rites, has been stressed for the above-described matrix as well, by arguing that it is those people that make up the interface between its two halves (Ibid:3; 7).

1.3 Material Culture

Of course, rites do not only involve people, they also involve things. Ranging from an old church building enhancing recursivity to a wooden cross being used as a symbolic focus, and from baptismal water enhancing performativity to a microphone enabling communication, objects are an integral part of any ritual activity. But what precisely is that part, and more importantly, how can it be analysed? One of the most fundamental ideas that has been put forward is that of object biography, as discussed by Igor Kopytoff in his highly influential article 'The cultural biography of things: commoditization as process' (Kopytoff 1986). Calling the modern Western polarity between thought and thing both recent and exceptional, he argues that it is worthwhile to ask the same questions of things as we ask of people (Ibid: 64; 66). That way a whole range of biographies can be studied, ranging from the physical to the economic and from the technical to the social. If one would want to make these biographies cultural however, special attention should be given to the object as a culturally constructed entity, with culturally specific meanings and classifications (Ibid: 68). This can be done for example by studying how actual objects achieve the biographical possibilities offered by a society and how this relates to a culture's idealised object biographies (Ibid: 66).

In following this notion of object biography, the idea that objects have lives, has become one of the fundamental concepts of material culture studies (Woodward 2007:31). And since these lives unquestionably involve human beings doing things with objects as well as doing things because of objects, there could be said to be a certain type of intersubjectivity, the study of which could prove worthwhile (Ibid:172). Because of this intersubjectivity, objects become part of culture, and in doing so objects can carry values and emotions. However, since they are not mere representations but also have a physical presence, they can also stand in for human beings. As a consequence of the latter, objects can gain social relationships with these human beings (Dant 1999:1-2; Dant 2005:4). But how are these relationships constituted? First of all, because of their physicality, objects have a performative dimension: people do things with and because of objects, and the things they do are of great consequence to their identity. Secondly, objects are talked about by those people, and through such narratives they acquire social positions (Woodward:151-2). In other words, the reason that we can speak of the life of objects is because they are *"are in a sense animated by their passage through the lives of people"* (Graves-Brown 2000:5). Of course various types of relations exist, as some objects remain environment and are only interacted in, such as rooms or parks, others are directly interacted with, such as doors and books, and yet others are interacted through, such as scissors or mobile phones (Dant 2005:6). These three types of relationships have increasing opportunities of becoming social, ranging from merely being of passive influence in social matters to the degree that the object itself can become seen as an actant, a thing with the possibility to socially act (Woodward 2007:15). However, the types of relationship that any object could acquire during its life, is neither inherent in its design, nor static throughout time but can change depending on its context and changes thereof (Dant 1999:131; Dant 2005:2; 4).

Given that much more time is daily spent interacting with objects than with other people (Dant 1999:15) and that these relations can be of social influence as discussed above, it follows that objects are not only shaped by, but are also shaping, social forms such as institutions, modes of interaction, beliefs and rituals (Ibid:12). In this way culture is both created and lived through material objects, and studying the way in which these things carry out social functions, regulate social relations and give meaning through the way they act upon people, as well as are acted upon by them, can inform us of such social forms (Woodward 2007:3-4). In studying the ways in which the material world thus shapes both individuals as well as cultures, care has to be taken that a simple causal or determinist viewpoint is not adopted by losing sight of the intricate mutuality between the way in which material culture shapes people and the way in which people shape material culture (Graves-Brown 2000:1-2). Conversely, overextending the focus on the latter process, by which objects become nothing more than materialisations of pre-existing cultural thoughts, is an equally over-simplistic reiteration of the mind-matter dichotomy. In an attempt to bridge precisely that Cartesian divide, the archaeologist Colin Renfrew introduced the idea of 'material engagement' as a unifying relationship between the thinking person and the material object (Renfrew 2005:23). In elaboration of this idea of material engagement, Lambros Malafouris, a student of Renfrew, proposed a new extended concept of cognition whereby material engagement is the "*synergistic process by which, out of brains, bodies and things, mind emerges*" (Malafouris 2005:58). This not in order to deny the existence of mental processes, but to argue that these are not primary to object-involving action but the dynamic and temporary outcomes of such encounters (Ibid:60). To complement this reasoning, Carl Knappett, another student of Renfrew, pointed out an interesting connection to James J. Gibson's concept of 'affordances', being an object's potentialities for certain actions (Knappett 2005:43-4). Gibson himself, in his influential work 'The Ecological Approach to Visual Perception', explained that the difference between the environment's measurable qualities and its affordances lies in the fact that the former pertain solely to the environment itself, while the latter are relative to the animal[6] undertaking a specific action (Gibson 1979:128). Water, for example, is stand-on-able for certain insects, but not for elephants. Affordances thus deal with the complementarity of the environment and animals (Ibid:127). According to Gibson, what an animal perceives when it looks at something, are not its qualities, but the whole of its affordances. And it does so directly, without having to classify or label it on the basis of pre-existing values or meanings (Ibid:134; 140). It is because of this last point, where Gibson starts

---

[6] Note that Gibson uses the word animal in a broad sense that includes human beings, while using the term environment to denote everything external to the animal.

moving towards a materialist determinism, that Knappett argues for a more moderate post-Gibsonian viewpoint, by introducing the idea of an affordance's transparency. What this means is that in any particular case it will be more or less transparent what an object's affordances are so that some will illicit immediate and unmediated reactions, while others will first be evaluated before being acted upon (Knappett 2005:46-8). Knappett underlines two other important aspects of affordances, namely that they are relational properties that may change according to the situation and that they will always contain a social component (Ibid:46-7). Thus coming full circle, one might wonder what types of affordances would be relevant for the understanding of ritual objects. Although focused strongly on North American Christianity, Colleen McDannell's work 'Material Christianity' was one of the first, and regrettably still one of the only, theoretical works that elaborated on the intersection of religion and material culture. Using the anthropologist Robert Armstrong's concept of 'affecting presence', she tried to establish ways in which religious objects were enlivened[7] in such a way that they became influential (McDannell 1995:18). She found four: by participation in the authority of institutional traditions, by creating and maintaining relationships with supernatural beings, by embodying memory and by binding people to each other (Ibid:18; 25; 39; 45). Interestingly it could be argued that the first and third way could be called recursive, while the second pertains to canonical communication and the fourth to communal symbolism, which would indicate the possibility of using the four aspects of ritual as types of affordances.

1.4 Theoretical Tools

Coming back to the question asked at the beginning of the introduction, the Allerzielen Alom celebrations as described there could be called a form of implicit religion, an integrating focus where imagination gained such credibility that it could, at least momentarily, help stave of the ontological insecurity brought on by people's encounters with the finitude of life. It could also be hypothesised that the ritual-like nature of the things going on are important, as the effective ambiguity of such activities help the

---

[7] Note that by discussing the way in which objects attain such affecting presences, McDannell is actually moving away from the way the concept is used by Armstrong himself, where only certain objects have affecting presences, that are intrinsic results of design and manufacture (e.g. Armstrong 1971: 24-5; 31-3).

celebration in gaining credibility, especially in lieu of any long standing tradition. It can be expected therefore that if those involved with Allerzielen Alom would want to enhance this effect, that one way they would do so is by more strongly ritualising it. This could be done either by directly making aspects of the celebrations more performative, communicative, recursive and symbolic, or by deliberately changing its context in ways that have such an increase as a consequence. In both cases the decisions of the people involved would be the critical interface between change and effect. However, because these decisions involve not only these people but also their material engagement with objects, and because of the intricate mutuality between the way in which material culture and people shape each other in such an engagement, it could be expected that the objects influence the outcome of these decisions.

As it is this possibly influencing role that is the subject of this thesis, theoretical tools are needed to analyse it. Specifically, terminology is needed that helps to answer the question in a graded and discriminating manner. The main concept adopted here for that purpose is that of affordances. Because, by looking at the practical, social and ritual relations afforded by material culture, in conjunction with the way in which the people involved deal with these affordances, the various manners in which objects matter can be more clearly elucidated. This entails looking at the various ways in which objects are interacted in, with or through during their uselife, as well as the performative, communicative, recursive and symbolic roles it can and/or does afford. But first the Allerzielen Alom case will have to be more thoroughly introduced, discussed and analysed.

Chapter Two:

Introducing Allerzielen Alom

In his book "Deeply into the Bone", Ronald Grimes describes the way in which the dead in the Western world are removed from everyday activity, and too much speaking about or with them is frowned upon, as a societal problem that is to be addressed by imaginative ritual inventing of new death rites (Grimes 2000:268). This concept of death rites, as he uses it, is broader than that of the funeral, as it also includes such things as preparation of the body, anticipating death and commemoration of the dead. (Ibid:222) The latter can be continued long after the actual death, and sometimes will not even be related to a specific death, for example during calendrical or seasonal commemorations of the dead in general. Such general commemorations can at the same time also function to help anticipate death as contact with the dead unavoidably evokes thoughts regarding one's own mortality (Ibid:254). To reintroduce such ideas pertaining to our dealings with the dead in the West he even talks of an *"urgency for us to lay hands upon them"* (Ibid:281). Although primarily meant in a literal sense, the idea is later elaborated upon in more symbolic terms, saying that for such a celebratory dwelling with the dead not only a specific space and time is needed but also *"myths and images that support communication with the dead"* (Ibid.) For this type of ritual communication it would already be enough to engage in tactile rites of talking and eating with the dead as if they were present, or only so in memory, imagination or as a visual icon, since belief does not actually seem to be a requirement. (Ibid:280-2). It is precisely this type of ritual creativity that seems to be presently developing in the Netherlands, where death is a subject that is very much alive, as the members of the 'Refiguring Death Rites' research group of the Radboud University of Nijmegen put it (Bolt, Heesels & Venbrux 2008:9). In their ongoing research they have already come across various new forms for death rites, which, in reaction to dissatisfaction with the traditional religious ritual repertoire, are less clearly bound, more fluid and multiform. The resulting ritual bricolages, which are inspired by contact with non-western religions as well as the elaborate funerals of famous Dutchmen and women, more often than not have a strong focus on the biography of the deceased (Ibid:10-1). In this chapter, that introduces Allerzielen Alom by discussing its initial development, it will become clear that this phenomenon can be seen as a reaction to the issue described by Grimes as well as being part of the larger trend described by the 'Refiguring Death Rites' research group.

2.1 Allerzielen Allicht and Herinnering Verlicht

Even before she started her All Souls' Day projects, rituals of departure had already been a part of Ida van der Lee's artistic repertoire through various works that dealt with the demolishment of old housing estates (Van der Lee 2008:21-2). When a female friend told her about experiences with All Souls' Day in Rome, where poetry and music were being performed at a cemetery, she got inspired and kept seeing the image of a lively and illuminated graveyard in her mind's eye (Ibid:22). Further inspiration was found in an online text by Cees van der Pluijm that described a vision of a Dutch All Souls' Day celebration that was similar to those in Mexico. As with these Días de los Muertos, the vision described the graveyard as busy and joyful with people clearing the graves, decorating them with flowers, and staying at the graveside with the whole family, throughout the night. Although Van der Lee did not consider everything equally applicable to the Dutch context, especially such things as the abundant use of skeletal imagery, it was the idea of death as being part of life instead of instilling fear, which made the text an appropriate script for the celebrations she had in mind (Ibid). Besides those of Mexico and Italy, the All Souls' Day celebrations of Poland and Spain have also been mentioned as inspirations as these also consist of more than just "*a visit to the grave with flowers and a candle*[8]" (Van der Lee 2007:Wat-Gedachtegoed-Tradities). In addition Van der Lee has pointed out that the tradition of All Souls' goes back in time way before the Catholic celebrations, to the time of the Celts who used it to adjure the falling of night and thus death (Ibid).

With these various inspirations in the back of her mind Van der Lee started organising Allerzielen Allicht[9] in 2005. This first year

---

[8] All translations are by the author.
[9] Literally meaning 'All Souls' Of Course' but can also be taken to mean 'All Souls' All Light'.

wasn't easy, first of all because of the difficulty in finding funds that were not put of by the taboos surrounding death, and secondly because of the difficulty in finding artists that would lend themselves for the concept (Van der Lee 2007:22). However, after several months of experimenting in a especially designated part of De Nieuwe Ooster memorial park[10], which had also been found willing to host the event, and through very hard work of both the artist and the park's personnel, the first celebrations were quite a success with about 1500 visitors, spread out over two nights (Van der Lee 2007: Wat-Ontwikkelingen 2005-2009). This first celebration was primarily meant as an 'trial and error' type experiment to see whether the concept would work and whether there would be any public interest, although the latter was clearly confirmed, regarding the former several lessons were learnt. The one-to-one collaboration between artists and bereaved, for example, turned out to be too exclusive, and the resulting art forms were to professional to serve as the examples they were meant to be (Van der Lee 2008:22). However, the art forms aimed at collective commemoration of the dead, whether buried at De Nieuwe Ooster or not, turned out to be quite effective as they provided the visitors the opportunity to perform small ritual acts. At the park's urn-pond, for example, people could release a small ceramic bowl containing lights and the name of the deceased into the water (see figure 1), which, besides making a beautiful display, made the symbolic act of letting go possible. (Ibid:25)

The next year, even though the initial idea had been too have Van der Lee organise a couple of celebrations after which De Nieuwe Ooster would continue on a much more modest scale, De Nieuwe Ooster decided to organise the celebration on their own under a new name: Herinnering Verlicht[11]. The split was the result of a difference of opinion on two points[12], the first being that whereas art was perceived as being primary for Van der Lee, De Nieuwe Ooster wanted to primarily focus on the bereaved they as a company were involved with. Secondly there was the point of art vs. practicality, with De Nieuwe Ooster wanting more control over decisions so as to somewhat limit the amount of time invested and more strictly structure planning to prevent last minute changes. On

---

[10] Originally the Nieuwe Ooster Cemetery, but nowadays called a memorial park due to the addition of a crematorium, scattering fields, urn-walls, an urn-pond, a bar and funeral museum 'Tot Zover' or 'This Far'.
[11] Which could be translated as 'Remembrance Enlightens', 'Remembrance Illuminated' as well as 'Remembrance Made Lighter'.
[12] The below is from personal communication with Carla van Elst on the 30th of June, 2009.

Fig. 1: Floating Lights at De Nieuwe Ooster. Photograph by Gabriella Hengeveld.

Fig. 2: Flag Tree at De Nieuwe Ooster Photograph by Maurice van der Molen.

a material level this meant discussions regarding such things as wanting storm lights, instead of the self made lights that Van der Lee considered to be more authentic fire, but which the people of the memorial park considered to be too prone to being blown out by the wind. It was these 'basic things' like illumination and routes that De Nieuwe Ooster wanted to be both simpler and more secure, rather than artistic. For the Floating Lights described above, this meant using round plastic cups instead of the square ones designed by one of the artists working with Van der Lee, and for the routing this meant limiting it to only one route instead of Ida's multiple ones. Another new development were the personal invitations going out to all who had someone buried or cremated at De Nieuwe Ooster, but which also carried the name of several cooperating companies so that they would work cheaper. Interestingly, because of their focus on the company's own community of bereaved as well as on practicality, these invitations could be seen as the material expression of the reasons behind De Nieuwe Ooster's decision to continue on their own terms. In addition to these changes, new forms for collective commemoration were also developed, such as writing messages on the paper surface of Thai Sky Lanterns, which were subsequently released, thus colourfully illuminating the night's sky. And in collaboration with the artist Jan van Schaick, the idea of a flag-tree was developed, where people could write a name on a ribbon and throw it into the tree while a choir was singing that same name (see figure 2). Although well visited, with one thousand visitors on one evening, it was not as well visited as the following year when many people, full of emotions, called others to convince them to come as well, and in the end four thousand visitors were counted. That year they also handed out small candles with paper holders so that people could walk around with them. The idea had come from Bert Hilhorst, a sacristan working in conjunction with De Nieuwe Ooster, and was inspired by the candles used in processions in Lourdes, although here the name of the celebration and the logo of the park were put on the paper holder instead.

2.2 Allerzielen Alom

Where the 2007 celebration organised by Van der Lee was an experiment to see whether the concept would work and garner interest, the 2008 celebrations, now under the name Allerzielen Alom, were a test to see how the concept would work in different contexts and locations (Van der Lee 2007: Wat-Ontwikkelingen 2005-2009). Because of the fact that more parties were found willing to contribute, in part due to the earlier success, it was possible to organise celebrations at five different locations in the province of Noord-Holland. The locations were chosen in conjunction with one of the funds 'Kunst en Cultuur Noord-Holland' so as to gain a broad spectrum of different locations, with the cemetery of Blaricum being placed in a wood and heath environment, that of Castricum next to the dunes, the Zorgvlied cemetery in urban Amsterdam and that of Purmerend no longer being in active use. Finally Schagen was deemed interesting because it would be the only one in the northern part of the province, and because it concerned a crematorium instead of a cemetery (Van der Lee 2008:25). Together with her curator Jaap Velsterboer, Van der Lee's main task was to guide the various artists and guard the overall tone and image. In her own words this meant a constant navigation *"between contradictions such as: theatre and reality, light and darkness, ethics and aesthetics, intimacy and publicity, being servient and being self-willed"* (Ibid). At each of the locations this navigation had a different thematic focus:

As the Zorgvlied cemetery is also a city park, with a flowing pattern in its paths, its main theme became the idea of a pearl necklace, with an illuminated path leading from pearl to pearl, each of these being a circular clearing where something special happened or could be done (Van der Lee 2007: Waar-2005-2007-Amsterdam Zorgvlied). An art form inspired by this location was the fire circle designed by Reinier Kurpershoek, where the bereaved could write the name of their dearly departed and hand it over to two vocalists who would sing this name, after which the name could be burned in the fire circle and go up through an illuminated column of smoke. Another, less interactive, example were the paraffin statues designed by Alphons ter Avest (see figure 3) and at the back of the cemetery Het Hiernamaals[13] was put up (see figure 4). In this collaboration of various artists, the illusion of 35 rooms was created with hay bales and crates and in each a sign was put up describing the room or its intended inhabitants in poetic terms such as 'room for mildly tempered' or room of anger, where people smoke'. Visitors were then to carefully choose a room to place a candle in for their dearly departed (Van der Lee 2008:82). At the exit of the cemetery a more homely spot was laid out with food, light projections and Passiepost[14] where people could craft and send a unique post card

---

[13] Dutch for The Afterlife.
[14] Dutch for Passion Post.

Fig. 3: Paraffine Statues in Castricum. Photograph taken by Max Linsen (2007).

Fig. 4: Hiernamaals in Castricum. Photograph taken by Max Linsen (2007).

so as to share their experiences with fellow bereaved that were not present (Ibid).

Since Blaricum is an artist-village, with a noticeable amount of personalised grave monuments, the chosen theme there was portraits, which meant a special focus on giving workshops so that people would be stimulated to create special ambiences around these monuments, while filmed portraits would be projected between the trees (Van der Lee 2007: Waar-2005-2007-Blaricum). In addition to these more personalised art forms, there were also several spaces for collective commemoration, such as Het Hiernamaals, that was put up just outside the cemetery itself (Ibid).

In Castricum, meanwhile, the main characteristic was an excursion into the dark dunes. Lights and guides led people by portraits projected on thins slates of ice to Het Hiernamaals, while a further trip up the Papenberg guided by soundscapes was optional (Ibid: Waar-2005-2007-Castricum). At the graveyard itself there were several things to be seen and done, either organised by people themselves or artists. One example of the latter were the Herinnerdingen[15], a project by Maaike Roozenburg. The original intention was that a wall would be formed of small crates, open to one end, each of which would have been decorated beforehand by the bereaved with objects of a deceased loved one[16]. However, since there was a lack of interest in displaying treasured objects in such a way, the decision was made to buy various second-hand objects that could be chosen by visitors on the basis of associated memories and then placed, together with a name or small message, in the wall, making the end-result both more interactive and more collective than initially intended (see figure 5).

Since the cemetery in Purmerend had not been used for 35 years, the focus there could be placed less on the individual deaths and the associated bereaved and more on a more universal form of commemorating. As a result the identity of the town became a focal point, with as its most characteristic feature a collective procession to the cemetery, to place the old cattle market to rest (Ibid: Waar-2005-2007-Purmerend).

For Schagen the special challenge was to design something that would compensate for the lack of graves, so that more personalised commemoration could still be made possible. Hereto Reinier Kurpershoek designed small sheds that people could use as a sort of personal relic cabinets (Van der Lee 2008:86). Another art form,

---

[15] A pun contracting the words herinneringen (remembrances) and the word dingen (things).
[16] From personal communication with Ida van der Lee on the 16th of July, 2009.

Fig. 5: Herinnerdingen. Photograph taken by Max Linsen (2007).

Fig. 6: Planted flower bulbs in Schagen. Photograph taken by Max Linsen (2007).

designed for the very windy Schagen was a line of white laundry on which relationships were printed in black such as father, colleague or lover. These were then to inspire people to think of other people to commemorate as well (Ibid:84).

Testing the various art forms in different locations taught Van der Lee some valuable lessons such as that the cemetery could be seen as reflection of the local community and that while each location's lay-out served as inspiration for different art forms, these art forms could, with a little repositioning, be used at other locations as well (Ibid:26). The laundry from Schagen, for example, was used at the other locations as well, and in fact on the evening in question the wind was completely calm in Schagen itself[17]. That being said, the response to these various forms were very different for the five locations. The Herinnerdingen for example worked quite well in both Castricum and Schagen, while the poetry used in Het Hiernamaals was much less popular in the latter than at Zorgvlied and in Blaricum where people were endlessly searching for just the right room to place their candle in. Although placing could have been a factor there as well, since Het Hiernamaals might have been placed to much out of the picture in Schagen. And while the people in Blaricum turned out to be much less willing to share their own personal commemorations with the wider community than expected, it was precisely this type of 'at the graveside' commemoration that turned out to be popular in Castricum. All in all however the celebrations were well visited, with a total of four thousand visitors (Van der Lee 2008:32).

2.3 A Website and a Booklet

In 2008 Van der Lee published a booklet entitled Allerzielen Alom, Kunst tot Herdenken'[18], reflecting on the success of the 2007 celebrations and discussing the background of the project, as well as its goals and underlying philosophy (Van der Lee 2008). In addition the project has its own website, where similar topics are presented as well. There, for example, it is explained that Allerzielen Alom is a multidisciplinary art project that aims to make the mystery of death manageable by giving it its own place in everyday life. Hereto artists help the bereaved in turning emotions and memories into image, text or sound. In this way an old tradition is

---

[17] This and the following is from personal communication with Ida van der Lee on the 16th of July, 2009.
[18] Meaning 'Art to Remember'.

recaptured to create a new contemporary ritual in which the dead are not kept silent about, but celebrated for who they were and what they can still tell us (Van der Lee 2007: Wat-Gedachtegoed). On this point Van der Lee writes in the booklet that while such a celebratory disposition towards the dead seemed a taboo, there turned out to be a need for it (Van der Lee 2008:21). Thus, given the success of the 2005 and 2007 celebrations and the recurring request for repetition Van der Lee deemed it important to transform Allerzielen Alom even more into a rite that could be passed on, so that every year, each and every municipality or funeral company can reconfigure their cemeteries into hospitable meeting places for the living where art can trigger their imagination into commemorating their dead in their own way (Ibid:21).

Hereto the booklet does not only discuss the celebration's background but also provides an elaborate overview of all the celebration's segments, art forms and decorative elements. People can let themselves be inspired by these examples and the many colour photographs accompanying them, and in most cases use them without fear of copy and/or image rights. Alternatively, those interested can make a choice of the available segments and invite a tender for Van der Lee and her foundation to organise the celebration for them (Ibid:76). Roughly speaking Van der Lee distinguishes three different levels for transforming the location, namely decorating the graveyard as a whole, creating places for active collective commemoration and the decorating of individual graves by the bereaved (Ibid:26-8). The purpose of decorating the graveyard as a whole is to make visitors feel welcome while showing them that this evening is unlike others. This means plotting a route with fire-baskets, lanterns, storm candles or even electric lighting, having guides present to show people the way and otherwise stand by people when needed, using or designing means of lighting for the specific locations where people can do or see things, designing decorative light forms to create a special atmosphere, handing out little bags with a small electric light to guide the way as well as candles and small lanterns that can be used by people to decorate graves with, having different types of appropriate live instruments being played throughout the cemetery, and finally having a place to make and eat some soup, soul bread or to drink some hot drinks together (Ibid:26; 76-80). To further enhance the special atmosphere artists can carefully contemplate, design and place art forms that express inner moods in a way that touches people, such as the named laundry, the paraffin statues and the projections of images on ice, already mentioned above (Ibid:84-6). Secondly, for the locations where active and collective commemoration are made possible, various art forms are described such as the Herinnerdingen, Het Hiernamaals, Passiepost and the Fire Circle and Floating Lights alluded to above as well as a Wensenkabinet[19] where people could place their wishes in hollow bamboo sticks and a place to bury flower bulbs (see figure 6), like the one described at the beginning of the introduction (Ibid:80-82). Van der Lee calls the things made possible at these locations 'small unforced ritual acts' whereby the dead are sounded, let go of or given a place and thus temporarily brought to the here and now (Ibid:28). Finally the decoration of individual graves and the organisation of small activities at the gravesides are deemed important as they help the cemetery come alive. Hereto introductory meetings can be scheduled to explain to visitors what the idea behind Allerzielen Alom is, possibly with the additions of workshops given by artists to teach people practical but alluring ways of decorating the grave, and a list is given with tips to bereaved such as arranging what is needed for a comfortable, warm and dry stay at the graveside, using photographs, text or clothing, or serving the deceased's favourite meal or drinks, listen to his or her favourite music or play the game he or she so liked (Ibid:86-8). Although all of these ideas and things can be used by whomever is inspired, Van der Lee has formulated one restriction on the website, namely that in order to use the protected Allerzielen Alom name, certain requirements have to be met such as that the celebration has to take place after dark in October or November, the location has to be illuminated and arranged in a hospitable manner, guides or hosts should be present as should be food and drinks, both the decoration of individual graves and the commemoration of people not buried or cremated at the location should be made possible, these possibilities should be clearly communicated beforehand, an informative introductory meeting has to be scheduled beforehand as well and all initiatives are to be made known to Van der Lee who has the final judgement regarding these restrictions (Van der Lee 2007: Wat-Gedachtegoed-Naam Allerzielen).

2.4 The Survey

Besides the information provided by Van der Lee herself, the booklet also contains two academic articles written by the members of the 'Refiguring Death Rites' research group: one of a more general

---

[19] Wishing Cabinet.

ethnographic nature, the other analysing the results of a survey held by the research group. In the former (De Maaker, Venbrux and Westrik 2008:59-70), the focus is mostly on impressions regarding the way Allerzielen Alom made it possible to experience the temporary presence of, and communication with, the dead in a personal manner but in conjunction with others. The contrast between light and dark or sound and silence, as well as the lay-out of the locations for collective commemoration and the sharing of food and drink are mentioned as material factors in providing this possibility (Ibid: 60; 65-7; 68). Another interesting comment is on the Christian origin of many of the material symbols used, such as fire, candles, crosses, classical singing and music (Ibid:68). Some of the findings discussed in the ethnographic article, such as the role of the collective in light of the individualisation of society and the role of people's religious in light of the secularisation, are studied in more quantified terms in the other article where a visitor profile is sketched as well. The article is the result of almost 400 surveys filled in by visitors after having been to Allerzielen Alom in 2007 (Quartier e.a. 2008:37-8), while a more elaborate presentation of their findings has been published in another article (De Maaker e.a. 2008). On the basis of the survey the following profile was created of the visitors (De Maaker e.a. 2008:160-5; Quartier e.a. 2008:38-45): 63.4% did not belong to any religious group, 27.7% were Catholic, 7.4% were Protestant and 1.5% belonged to another religious group. Regarding their ages 13.3% was under 40 years old, 50% between 40 and 60, while 36.7% was above 60. Of the visitors 17.3% came alone, 24.3% with a partner, 16.8% with one or more family members, 10.8 % with a friend and 30% with several people. The purpose of the visit for 44% of the visitors was the commemoration of several people, of a family member for 24.6%, of the dead in general for 10.9%, while only 6.4% came for non-commemorative reasons. The relationship to the deceased was described by 40.9% as very intensive, 25.1% as intensive, 16.9% as averagely intensive, 6.1% as superficial and 3.5% as very superficial. This means that among the visitors there was an above average amount of secularised people, the age-differentiation was less focused on the elderly than would be expected from the secularisation thesis and the celebrations' topic, many more people came *en groupe* than the individualisation thesis would predict and commemoration was the primary purpose of visiting, not the art or curiosity while the relationship to these deceased was on the whole intensive to very intensive.

In addition to the profile-questions, questions were also asked regarding the visitors' attitudes concerning certain issues, which had to be evaluated on a scale of 1 to 5 (Quartier e.a. 2008a:164-169). Some of the questions inquired after people's image of God, factor analysis of which showed a 3.1 evaluation of an anthropomorphic image of god, and a 3.6 evaluation of both a non-anthropomorphic image and a less clearly describable meta-image. Another set of questions pertained to the emotions that visitors had experienced, of which the factor analysis showed a 3.6 evaluation of positive emotions such as rest, warmth, comfort and togetherness and only a 0.9 evaluation of negative ones like solitude and powerlessness. Finally inquiry was made regarding the importance of remembrance and hope, both in religious/spiritual and personal terms. Here the factor analysis showed a 4.2 and a 4.1 evaluation of, respectively, personal remembrance and hope, a 3.0 and 3.3 evaluation of, respectively, religious/spiritual remembrance and hope, and only a 2.3 evaluation of no hope at all. This would mean that the average visitor doubted, but not rejected, an anthropomorphic image of God, thinking more in terms of a non-anthropomorphic or meta-image. Similarly religious/spiritual hope and remembrance was deemed less important than personal hope and remembrance, although here again there was no actual rejection of the former. Interestingly the forward looking attitude of hope was more highly evaluated than the backward looking attitude of remembrance when in religious terms, while being reversed in the more personal terms. Finally, the fact that no hope at all was much less strongly evaluated corresponds to the type of emotions that were being felt. In a recent presentation on Allerzielen Alom, Thomas Quartier, described the position of the celebration in relation the factors analysed above as that of a ritual pendulum finding a balance between such felt contradictions as continuity versus discontinuity, individuality versus collective and immanence versus transcendence (Quartier 2009). Ritual acts, because they are something that is done instead of something that is said can thus bridge these contradictions, at least, when properly guided (Ibid).

2.5 Discussion

From the above introduction to the Allerzielen Alom project it will be clear that it is a perfect case for the study of the role of material culture in emerging rites, as there is plenty of the former, while the latter is consciously aimed at. Additionally it is clearly a form of implicit religion in that the celebrations have proven to be highly successful integrating foci for dealing with human finiteness. Interestingly, the way this integrating is described by Quartier as the seeking of a balance between continuity and discontinuity, individuality and collectivity and immanence and transcendence sounds comparable to the four ritual aspects described in chapter one. With the bridging of the first contradiction being related to the idea of recursivity, the second to the way rites can be symbolic in both an individual and a communal sense and the third to the rite communicating messages referring both to the current situation as well as canonical truths. Finally, the idea of performativity is reflected in the fact that 'doing something' is mentioned as the main reason why a rite is capable of this balancing act in the first place. This, however, does not answer the question whether the role of material culture and its affordances is relevant to this continuous process. Of course several clues can be found in the descriptions given so far, but given that the affordances of material culture were described as relational and emergent, a more contextual look at the material culture is needed to come to an actual answer.

Chapter Three:

Visiting Allerzielen Alom

In 2008 not only De Nieuwe Ooster repeated its Herinnering Verlicht, but there were nine Allerzielen Alom celebrations as well, namely in Schagen, Groningen, Castricum, Alphen aan den Rijn, Amsterdam IJburg, Apeldoorn, Leeuwarden, Oostzaan and Winschoten. The first of these two were organised by Van der Lee and her project group, the third was organised by local volunteers who did not want the 2007 celebration to be a one time event, while the rest were new local initiatives on the basis of Van der Lee's booklet and organised under her guidance (Van der Lee 2007: Wat-Vieringen 2005 – 2008). Of these celebrations five were visited for small-scale ethnographic fieldwork, in order to gain a better sense of the various contexts in which material culture was placed and put to use[20]. In choosing the celebrations that were visited, an attempt was made to cover the various stages of development as well as the regional distribution, although the simultaneity of several of the celebrations severely limited choice. Groningen was chosen both because it was organised by Van der Lee herself and because it was located in the north, Castricum because it was the second time Allerzielen Alom would be celebrated at the location, De Nieuwe Ooster because it concerned their fourth celebration and because of its independent development and finally Alphen aan den Rijn and Apeldoorn were chosen to represent the new initiatives, because they were held in otherwise unvisited provinces. At each of the locations the primary focus was to witness and talk about the ways visitors related to the material culture that was involved. In Amsterdam and Castricum the secondary goal was seeing how people dealt with the fact that this was not the first time the

---

[20] Given that any participating-observer cannot but become part of the context of these situations under study, this necesitates the more personal and reflexive voice used here for describing them.

celebration was organised. The results of the five fieldtrips will be presented below in a chronological order.

3.1 Herinnering Verlicht in Amsterdam

As I arrived[21] at De Nieuwe Ooster before the celebration would start I could make a quick stroll through the typical 19th century memorial park, where I saw an old man tidying up a grave while employees and volunteers, recognisable through the yellow or red light bands on their arms, were busy with such last moment things as lighting the storm lanterns, fire baskets and fire bowls or putting up the benches for the piano players.

Once back at the gate I saw people arriving of all ages and various ethnicities, some coming with their family, others were evidently friends, while several were waiting for others to arrive. The two fire baskets present here were providing not only light and smell, but also some much needed warmth on this rather cold evening. As such they rapidly became focal points for the people present, who took the opportunity to make pictures of them, as well as of the entrance and each other. In front of the flower stall across the street a row was forming, and most people going through the gate had either flowers or a plant with them. Once in, people took a moment to study the map that was handed out to them (see figure 7), which explained that this year there would be no fixed route, although three differently coloured laser lights would shine over the main paths for guidance. Other people, meanwhile, were making photographs of the flame shaped fire constructions put up on the grass in front of the aula, or the words Herinnering Verlicht projected onto that same building. Next, most people walked through the aula, where one could drink coffee and tea, to the other side where the candles described in chapter two were lighted and handed out (see figure 8). The first thing grabbing one's attention here was the blue laser shining towards the aula, and most people slowly walked towards its origin. Slowly, because the candle that was just handed out to them was still struggling to keep burning, but also because of the serene, somewhat otherworldly atmosphere, created by the blue laser light, the almost waist-high white light balls placed on intervals across the path and the white, light-emitting, umbrellas of the Witte Dichters[22] that were available to read a poem to you, either there, or at the grave side. Other people

---

[21] The visit was made on Wednesday the 29th of Ocober, 2008.
[22] White Poets.

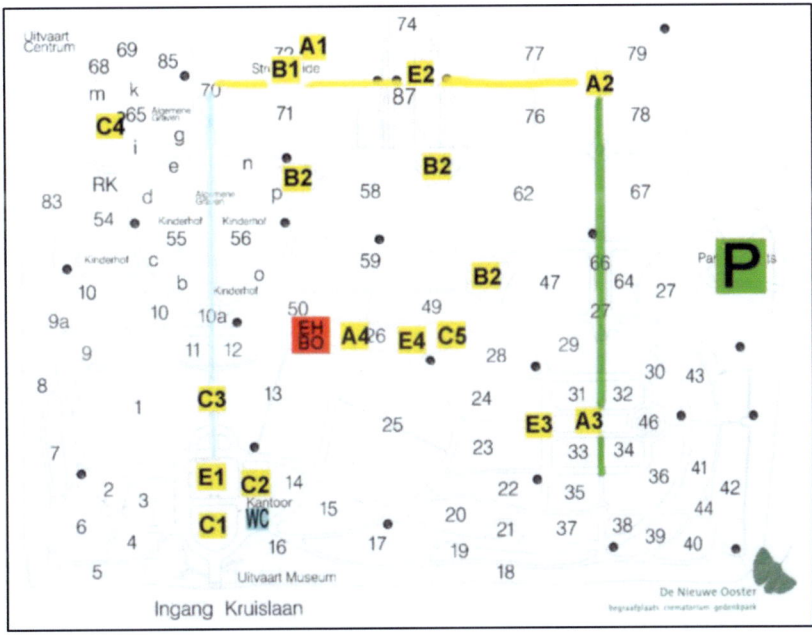

Fig. 7: Map handed out at Herinnering Verlicht 2008.

crossed the path, looking for a particular grave, and when they had found it, they carefully placed some flowers or plants and some tea lights, grave candles or the candle handed out to them on the grave, often staying for a while, in many cases making pictures of the now illuminated grave. At the end of this lane, most people made a short stop at another piece of fire-art, just to the left of the lane, then going to the right where a woman was telling a story about hope, and asked people to place a grave candle on the white lines laid out on the floors so that gradually a six-pointed star would emerge (see figure 9). Going on in the direction of the yellow laser beam, one could already hear the traditional Surinam funeral band play in the distance, but first one arrived at the urn pond, where, with the help of several volunteers, Floating Lights could be made. After having put the light to water, most people stared at it for a while, commenting on the beauty of all those lights together, and again, they made pictures. Going by the three storytellers, who were somewhat shielded of from their surroundings through the use of white sheets, and were located a bit of the main three illuminated lanes, I moved to the end of the green beam where people were sitting on a temporary stand, listening to two piano players. Close by, people could sit at a table to write messages on coloured Thai Sky Lanterns, the fire of which was then lighted while the various people who had contributed to it watched it go up, staying until it

Fig. 8: Walking with candles at De Nieuwe Ooster. Photograph taken by Johan Mullenders.

Fig. 9: Creating a star at De Nieuwe Ooster. Photograph taken by Gabriella Hengeveld.

was out of sight. Since the night was a bit moist the paper lanterns were not entirely steady, which created a bit of tension in the onlookers, followed by relief when all went well, and some disappointment the one time I saw it burst into flames and come down. I heard people commenting to each other that this was just as beautiful the year before. Coming finally to the central point of the park, where people could sit on benches around fire baskets while drinking hot wine or eating soup or looking at a screen on which the 2300 names of all those buried and cremated at De Nieuwe Ooster in the last year were projected, the mood was more outgoing than at other, more tranquil, parts of the cemetery. By the benches two almost man-high wooden tripods were set-up, with candles and incense in the middle, and small holes in its beams. Without any guidance, people lighted some incense and placed it in a hole and I even heard two people asking each other what they had wished for. The long list of names seemed to make quite an impression, and again people made pictures when a known name came by. When a name was absent this led to some consternation, and a notation of it was made in the guestbook. This same book was also used by people to either express gratitude for the magical atmosphere, to state how many times they had already been at the celebration before or, in the majority of cases, to note down the names of those that had been commemorated, often directing their message at those very deceased. While standing by the guestbook I talked with several people, such as a woman who had already gone to the grave of her twin brother in the afternoon so that she would not arrive at a dark grave and a middle-aged man expressing that he didn't care what else would change in the world, as long as this would remain, if need be, people should just make some donations! Many of the visitors I talked to also had things to say on what had been beautiful again, like the Floating Lights, and what had been missing this year, such as the flag-tree. When leaving at the end of the celebration I heard an employee tell Carla that five thousand candles had been handed out, and close to the gate I saw that many of them had been placed, still burning, in the large flower tubs as well as in the flower beds.

3.2 Allerzielen Alom in Alphen aan den Rijn

When I arrived at the gate of the Oosterbegraafplaats in Alphen aan den Rijn, it was still closed and a volunteer explained that it would be opened later so that everybody could enter together. An exception was made for me, however, so I could meet Hedi

Hegeman, the ritual guide whose initiative this celebration was. From her I received some matches to light any not-yet burning lights and a small scoop that I had to deliver at the memorial circle at the end of the main lane, where the flower bulbs would be planted. At the left of this lane, grave candles were placed every few meters, while a string of electric lighting, rather strongly, illuminated the right side. Where the broader paths branched of, grave candles were placed as well, while these same candles, together with fire baskets and at the meeting point an industrial lamp, illuminated the places for collective commemoration. On many of the graves lights were already burning as well and volunteers were busy with the last preparations.

Returning outside I noticed there was an atmosphere of anticipation, probably due to having to wait outside. The visitors, as far as I could see, were all Caucasian, but, again of various generations, and while many seemed to be family, others were clearly friends. As in Amsterdam they carried flowers and plants, as well as candles and lanterns, some of the latter already burning. Many people also had umbrellas with them as it had already rained, and more rain was predicted. Unlike in Amsterdam, nobody was taking pictures, a trend that continued through out the evening as far as I could tell. Even before the volunteer was done opening the gate, people were already flocking together, however, once inside only one woman was handing out programs/maps (see figure 10), thereby preventing a rushed entry. People were then told to go to the meeting point, a triangular field of grass, next to which chocolate milk was being handed out. Once people received their drink and had taken place at one of the three sides of the triangle, with the one closest to the chocolate milk being the most popular, Hedi opened the celebration with a poem about light. Next, she explained the goal of the evening, which, although being called after a Catholic feast day, was intended for everybody and described the activities possible at each location for collective commemoration. In the coffee room people could have their music played, receive glow sticks and ask for directions to a grave, next to the meeting point people could place a wish in hollow sticks or a small tree, buy roses for the graves or place candles or commemorative objects at the triangle of grass, on the Catholic segment of the cemetery young people could take place in discussions on pillows around a fire basket, at the so-called Kindervlinder[23] children could play with clay or paint or let up some balloons and finally, at the memorial

---

[23] Meaning Children's Butterfly, being the butterfly shaped section of the cemetery where the children's graves are located.

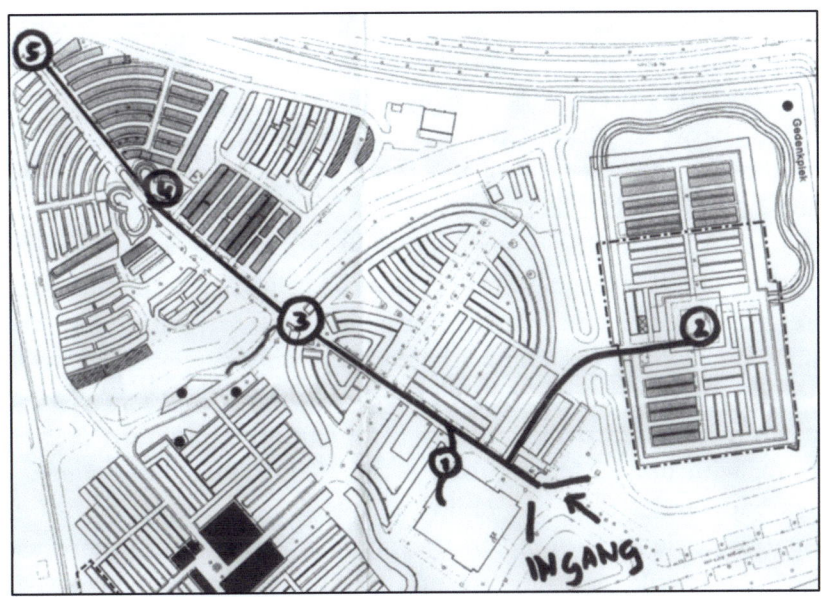

Fig. 10: Map handed out in Alphen aan den Rijn 2008.

Fig. 11: A Thai Sky Lantern.
Photograph by Hedi Hegeman.

circle, flower bulbs could be planted, poetry read and music played, mantras would also be sung there later on the evening. After the explanations two slow spiritual dances, named Balance and Light, were danced by a dance group, with a poem about the soul being read in between. When the microphone for the poem did not immediately work, several of the roughly two hundred visitors left. When I left as well, I saw that most people were busy going to the graves and decorating them. Although they also walked by the chocolate stand where several options for collective commemoration were grouped, they mostly did not actually do anything more than glance at it, and at the end of the evening, only some candles could be found on the triangle of grass. Others had a quick look at the exposition of musical instruments and Christian/Eastern spiritual objects, with only a few lighting some of the available incense. At the Kindervlinder only one child was playing with clay. But at the memorial circle at the end of the main lane, however, there were about fifty people standing around, talking or keeping warm at the fire basket, while others were busy planting flower bulbs, with somebody shining a flashlight to help them. Various types of 'the deceased's favourite music' were played and a lady recited some poems. By the time the mantras started, however, most people had already gone to the very brightly lid coffee room to drink some coffee, tea or wine and fill in the survey lying on the tables. I sat next to a 63 year old man who had not planned to come, but decided to bring his wife because of the rain and the fact that the street lanterns along the road to the cemetery were malfunctioning. He had not really liked the spiritual dancing or the mantras, but he did like the three white Thai Sky Lanterns that I apparently missed (see figure 11). He and his wife had also burned some candles at the grave of his wife's family and planted a flower bulb for her father, whose grave had been located elsewhere and had already been emptied. He himself had picked up a leaf to take home with him, from the tree under which the ashes of some of his family members had been scattered.

3.3 Allerzielen Alom in Groningen

Around the Yarden crematorium, which is located at the edge of the city of Groningen, there is a memorial park with some woodland, three ponds, a scatter field, a section with urn graves and a columbarium. When sitting by the gate of this crematorium I noticed that the make-up of the visitors was again comparable to those in Alphen aan den Rijn, only with much less young children. Despite some groups of torches standing in front of the gate, all of these visitors directly moved inside, where a carpet of dead leaves to stroll through was lain out and free candles were given out in the 'light shop' on the right. Most people went directly to the stand to choose either a grave candle, a small candle in a decorated glass or some electric or real tea lights. From here the route took the visitors into the woods on the right, and to make sure that people went this way and not towards the illuminated pond in front of them, a fence was placed, that was however not illuminated, causing at least one collision. In addition two people were standing at the edge of the forest to hand out paper bags illuminated by an electric tea light (see frontispiece). The rest of the way the route was made clear by torches and, further on, lanterns on tripods standing beside it. Interestingly, the paper bags did not make the visitors walk any slower, although the presence of large wooden letters making up words like Herinnering[24] besides the path did. The winding nature of the path and the surreally illuminated pond and bushes as well as the pictures taken thereof, also added to the calm of the place, despite the presence of a noisy highway nearby. On a few of the memorials located in these woods the candles handed out at the entrance could already be seen burning. Immediately upon leaving the woods a woman was sitting behind a table on which names could be written on paper slips that were then to be sung and burned as described in chapter two. Here people's strong emotions were already evident during the writing of the name, and by the time it was being sung, many tears could be seen. While some people remained standing, others sat on the small wooden stubs standing in a circle around the fire that was continuously being fed by the artist that designed it. From Daphne Questro, one of the two singers who also designed the repetitive and improvised mode of singing used here, I later learned that originally the singers burned the paper but that van der Lee changed this to increase interactivity. Meanwhile, in a corner of this scatter field, some visitors were busy decorating a spot for their dearly departed, the illumination of their candles was so bright however, that several people mistook it for the light indicating the route, which actually went the other way toward the flower bulb planting. There, one of the employees of the crematorium had already lighted the candles that were to be placed, together with a little text-flag, as an indication of the planted bulb. She told me that it was busy enough for her not to have to tell people what to do, as they could simply

---

[24] Which could be translated as both memory and remembrance.

imitate others. Emotions were still high here, although she told me of people laughing as well, for example because one of the deceased's famous quotes was put on the flag. Passing some benches where people could drink some hot chocolate people next arrived at the table where the Floating Lights could be made. When these Floating Lights were then placed in the water they floated away much farther than in Amsterdam, due to the size of the pond and a light breeze. This effect spontaneously created a sense of competitiveness in people who started commenting on the speed of various lights. One young woman, who was trying to make a picture of her light together with all the others, even exclaimed "He is being slow again!" The volunteer working here later told me of similar personal ways of referring to the lights, such as a woman who, when her light remained at the pond's edge, stated that "She cannot let go". On the other side of the pond another light shop, this one with small torches as well, was located just before on entered the urn-grave section of the crematorium's park. Many of these graves were by then already decorated with both candles and torches handed out here as well as those brought by people. At many of the graves, the candles had been carefully placed to make up a line, circle or other shape. At one grave people were still busy with decorating it for the perfect picture, and even one of the industrial lights illuminating a nearby tree was temporarily put to a different use to acquire it. When the trumpeter playing here had a short break, he told me that it was very different to play in this secluded section, where he could intimately address individual people, than the day before on a field in the rain in Schagen where he could go all out. After passing another pond, where people stopped to stare at another wooden word floating in the water, the visitors then entered the columbarium where the Herinnerdingen were displayed. I immediately noticed how little explanation was needed for people to begin making links between a coffee cup and father's fondness of coffee or a door handle and that one story about somebody ripping one of. Others saw a pile of numbers on small metal plates and start looking for number 14, which was 'his lucky number'. After being chosen, the objects, accompanied by the same colourfully illuminated plastic baskets used for the Floating Lights, were placed in the empty compartments of the urn-walls, thereby illuminating them. Unlike with the texts written on the papers used for the Floating Lights, the messages here were more or less put on display, together with the object. Some explained the choice of the object, others had small poems, while yet other were directed at the deceased, such as a woman explaining to her uncle why she hadn't been present at his sickbed and funeral. Most visitors not only placed an object in one of the compartments, but spend quite some time looking at others as well. Just outside of the columbarium a member of Van der Lee's project group, was busy pouring in hot wine and chocolate milk from an enormous pan, while people sat on hay bales drinking it. Here, the Passiepost was also located and while I sat at the table with other people decorating their card one woman told me she had come despite not having anybody here, instead she wanted to commemorate the dead in general, as in the heathen days.

3.4 Allerzielen Alom in Apeldoorn

Upon my arrival at the Soerenseweg cemetery in Apeldoorn it was already dark and I could see the two illuminated buildings flanking the gate loom up through the mist in the distance.[25] On the other side I briefly talked to Alinde Vrolijk, one of the three organisers of the celebration, who was having a quick dinner with the volunteers before the first visitors would arrive. When these did I saw the same types of visitors as in Alphen aan den Rijn, but here the gate was open, so most walked directly over to the light stand to pick up a grave candle, some tea lights or a torch. Here they were also given a map (see figure 12) with descriptions and one of the paper bags that were placed in curvy lines next to it. In it, there were two electric tea lights, one of which could be used to read the map, which most immediately started doing. From here the route, indicated by burning torches, followed the winding paths of the cemetery in such a way that most of the times other torches could be seen, through the mist, in the distance. When the path arrived at a crossroads, a semicircular line of electric tea lights was lain out to indicate the route. At random intervals small clusters of semi-transparent bags, with electric tea lights in them, were placed besides the paths for decoration. Multicoloured industrial lights illuminated certain trees as well as the party-tents that covered the locations for collective commemoration. At these places fire baskets, candles and torches also provided extra light and warmth. Due to the old trees, the winding paths, the anciency of the cemetery itself, and of course the mist, the atmosphere was quite tranquil and even somewhat mysterious. The fact that the route first led past a woman playing a harp and then to wooden letters spelling the word Herinnering, on which several people had placed small candles,

---

[25] The visit was made on Tuesday the 4th of November, 2008.

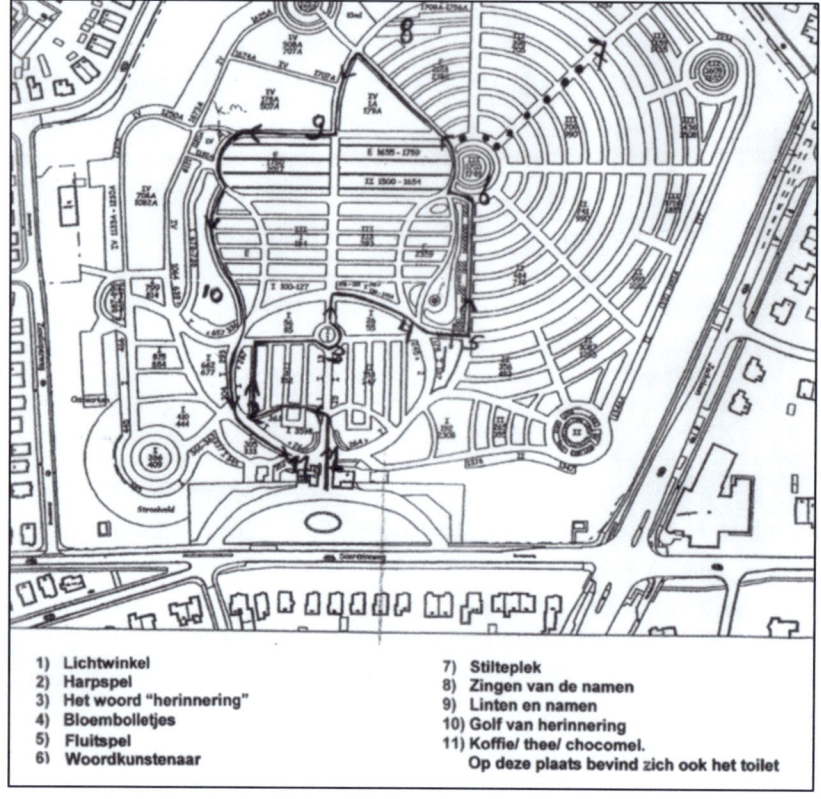

Fig. 12: Map handed out at Allerzielen Alom in Apeldoorn 2008.

Fig. 13: Hanging up Ribbons in Apeldoorn. Photograph taken by Ida van der Lee (2008).

only added to this mood. From this point to the place where the flower bulbs could be planted a short cut was possible, and although a fence was put up to indicate that the route went past it, it was not illuminated and largely ignored. While I stood looking by, a middle-aged couple planted a flower bulb and flag by the curvy cords lain out there to indicate the proper location. To him, she stated that it would be impossible to explain to anybody what the evening was like and he agreed that one would have to have seen it, although next year people could see the flowers. She then wondered if the person they had lost could see them, to which he replied that he definitely thought so. Coming by a man playing a Tibetan sound bowl, most people stopped to listen for a moment, before going on towards the Huis van Bezinning[26], a stand decorated by the poet Robert La Boresa, who was reciting short poems about waiting and about having to look for words. During these recitations he made use of various props such as a table with red wine and white bread or words on small plastic disks that he could hand out. Meanwhile a family came by, carrying several bags and even a white bucket, in search of particular graves. When I walked to the Stilteplek[27] a while later, I saw they had found them and were busy placing lights on them in a manner that was elaborately discussed. At the Stilteplek itself, the volunteer working there was discussing the evening with one of the visitors, while advising others to light up a tea light and place it on one of the wooden stubs. Besides the wooden stubs, the chairs had also been claimed by these lights already, so that nobody could actually sit on them. Returning back to the route from the Stilteplek, the next location for collective commemoration was located somewhat of the main path, although the names being sung there, lured people to it anyway. Here, the circle of light had been substituted by a fire basket and the burning of the name was mentioned only as an option. Later, Alinde Vrolijk, who was one of these singers, told me that frequently they made up a name to sing when they saw illuminated bags come by in the distance, so that people would know they were there. Further down the route a line was hung between two trees and people could choose a coloured ribbon to write a name or message on, which they then had to hang on the line to give it to the wind, as the woman standing by it called it (see figure 13). Hereafter the route led to the Golf van Herinnering[28], which consisted of a long bands of blue fabric, lain out in such a way as to suggest waves. Here

---

[26] Meaning House of Contemplation.
[27] Meaning Place of Silence.
[28] Meaning Wave of Remembrance.

people could choose an object, as with the Herinnerdingen, and place it, together with a small message on the fabric (see figure 14). Interestingly, even though the band was many meters long, only the first few meters were being used by people. Close by several families were decorating graves with candles and flowers, the children that were present being actively involved. Finally, coming back to the entrance, many of the visitors were standing around drinking some coffee or tea, as the chocolate milk had already been finished, and discussing the evening.

3.5 Allerzielen Alom in Castricum

After having introduced myself to Marina van der Wal en Raldi Beentjes[29], this year's organisers, I was immediately given the task to help light the torches that were already placed along all of the paths of the Onderlangs cemetery. Walking around, I saw that in addition to these torches, industrial lights had been put up to illuminate the trees as well as the various locations for collective commemoration. Some of the torches were difficult to light up, as the evening was very moist, with a bit of a drizzle. Many of the graves already had burning candles on them and one even had six burning torches. One family, consisting of a grandmother, her daughter and husband and their young son and daughter, was busy lighting torches on each side of the stone, rearranging a light string on the small hedge skirting the grave and lighting candles in the glass jars hanging from a nearby tree. When I talked to them they told me the grave was of the woman's younger brother and that they had already put everything in its place in the afternoon and were now lighting it all up. The small glass jars on the grave itself had been decorated by the children by gluing coloured snippets of paper on them., the largest one even said uncle on it. She told me that more people had decorated the graves than the year before, but they had done so as well last year, although in a different manner. Sitting by the entrance, after all torches had been lighted, I noticed that the atmosphere was very different. Two young ladies dressed in white sheets were putting multicoloured glow sticks around people's arms, while a man played the trumpet accompanied by two children with percussion instruments. As the two young women were apparently well known and the putting on of the glow sticks went none to quick, there were quite an amount of people waiting, enthusiastically conversing with friends and family. Among them

---

[29] The visit was made on Wednesday the 5th of November, 2008.

Fig. 14: Golf van Herinnering in Apeldoorn. Photograph taken by Ida van der Lee (2008).

Fig. 15: Herinnerdingen in Castricum. Photograph taken by Ida van der Lee (2008)

were much more young people and children than at the other locations, barring perhaps Amsterdam. Once in, people could and did go to both the left and the right, as there was no fixed route and the locations for collective commemoration were spread out over the cemetery. Several of these have of course already been mentioned in the introduction such as the messages that could be hung in one of two young potted trees and the planting of flower bulbs for which a whole still vacant lot of the cemetery's new section was available, although most tended to plant their bulb and flag on the edges anyway. Later on in the evening the two whitely clad volunteers standing by this post told me they had the feeling most people did not know they were there, except when the choir came by to sing at the columbarium. At the pond, which was close by, a woman was singing to a Tibetan sound bowl, while an elderly lady was handing out small wooden disks and rounded stones on which people could write a message or draw something. She told me that she hadn't been to the celebrations last year but had heard nice stories so when the advertisement came up for this year she volunteered to help. She also explained to me that her idea had been inspired by the fact that the ink of drawings placed on graves often runs but that she told people to with the disks as they pleased. Some of them had already been placed at a large stone standing by the pond, while others had decided to burn the disk instead. A version of the Herinnerdingen was also present, with the objects placed on a carrier cycle and a nearby table (see figure 15). The objects could not be put on display however, nor could messages be written, and although stories still came up, people tended to stay for a much shorter time, probably because they had nothing to write or read. Close by there was also a stand where a man was giving a workshop in painting and making poetry, which was especially popular with young children. At the poetry-doors described in the introduction, a man was playing a guitar while people walked in between the doors to read the poem or stood by one of the fire baskets to talk to friends or family. Finally, at the centre of the graveyard, room was made to drink hot wine or chocolate and sit on hay bales. Here, a light stand was also located.

The biggest distinction with the other celebrations was the amount of work that had gone into the decoration of the graves. This ranged from elaborately lighting the grave with candles, torches and tea lights arranged into shapes such as a heart to confiscating nearby benches to share food and drink with others coming by and from hanging names or pictures in small trees put on the grave to a man maintaining three fires near the small columbarium in which his wife had been placed. People also visited the graves of others either to talk with the bereaved or to discuss the way it had been decorated. Some graves were even more abundantly decorated, such as that of a teenage girl that had recently died in an accident. Her mother had created the illusion of a four-poster-bed with the use of some pink cloth, while her picture in a pink frame was placed on a small dais together with some candles decorated with butterflies and some golden necklaces. At the end of the evening I spoke to the woman as she was just cleaning up the cookies that had been placed on a small table nearby and she told me that the evening had done her good and that she would leave the candles burning as she could not bear the idea of leaving her behind in the dark. Another grave had been transformed into a winter landscape by two sisters to commemorate their parents who had met on an ice skating track. Hereto they had used a white piece of cloth to make the track and had hung white paper ice stars, cotton bowls and shower puffs from the surrounding trees. They served their parents' favourite drinks and the music they used to skated to played in the background. The spectacle triggered many people to ask them for an explanation and they were in conversation throughout the evening. When I talked to them, some family members came by to bring them an appropriately white candle and tell them of the rest of the cemetery as they didn't have the opportunity to see for themselves yet. One of the graves they mentioned was that of a father who had recently died, and in absence of a tombstone, his young son had spelled his name in tea lights. Later I learned from Marina that the boy had refused to leave the grave until all the candles had burned out. At the newest grave of the cemetery, three friends of the deceased woman were trying to let up a Thai Sky Lantern. When I came by to help them, it became apparent that they hadn't really seen the rest of the cemetery either, as one of them complained that last year was more symbolic and artistic and had involved such things as the Herinnerdingen and the planting of flower bulbs. In a similar vein I overheard many people comment on the absence of certain features, such as the Floating Lights, access to the dunes and the presence of illuminated paper bags.

3.6 Discussion and Analysis

When wanting to analyse the descriptions of the five celebrations given above, one enters into a murky and confusing web of interrelated factors that are all of influence on the shape and mood of the celebrations. These range from the evening's weather to the shape of the location and which parts of it were used and in what manner, and from the type of activities that were made possible to the amount and types of people involved both on the organising as on the visiting side. However, by looking at the various affordances of the objects involved, a way might be found through that complicated web so that at the very least their position in it can be made somewhat clearer. Hereto, some examples will be taken from the above, to look at the symbolic, recursive, communicative and performative affordances of these objects[30].

One example could be the illuminated paper bags that were handed out at the entrance in Groningen and Apeldoorn. One thing these paper bags afforded was visibility, although not so much of a person's surroundings, the light was too soft for that, but of the person itself, like with the singers in Apeldoorn who started singing as soon as they saw bags in the distance. Through actually carrying the bags, individuals communicated both their participation in the evening and their symbolic link to unknown others that like them carried such a bag, because the act of walking was now framed into the act of walking after others and in front of yet others. This procession of lights has of course a recursively Christian aspect to it, which is even clearer for the candles handed out in Amsterdam. The latter, although related to the illuminated bags, also have other ritual affordances as they could not only be carried, but also afford the performative act of placing. When this is done on a grave, this performance communicates a link between the bereaved and the deceased and in doing so maintain this bond without going having to explicitly justify it. But when the candles are placed in flower tubs at the exit they again communicate the coming together of individuals recursively symbolised by the individual candles. That the carrying of paper bags can very quickly become recursive as well however is evident from the statements in Castricum about their absence.

In addition to carrying lights, people were also following the torches and lanterns indicating a route through the dark. Although this might seem of little consequence in terms of ritual affordances, it is through their illumination that people are guided from one spot for collective commemoration to the other. They thereby help activate the affordances of the objects in these locations, which

---

[30] From the above descriptions numerous other examples could be analysed to come to roughly the same conclusions, but for the sake of brevity these have not been included.

would otherwise get ignored. That this is a matter of contrast was clear in Castricum where the planting of the flower bulbs got less attention as people were not led to them. Through the creation of contrast, the lights also communicate which areas are communal and which are private. To go to the latter, one literally has to bring light into the darkness, thereby adding a highly recursive light-dark symbolism to the above alluded to performative act of placing candles on a grave.

The Floating Lights is an interesting example as well because it demonstrates how ritual aspects are actually not the result of individual affordances, but of an interplay of affordances. Here we have water that affords floating to a plastic cup which affords carrying to a candle which affords visibility to coloured paper that affords recognition by a visitor. Since the paper also afforded writing and thus communication with the deceased, this relation is easily transformed into a symbolic identification between the deceased and the Floating Light. Consequentially the action of placing it in the water is framed as the symbolic act of letting somebody go, although the subsequent joining up with other such lights implicitly communicates a new coming together. At the basis of the symbolism communicated here are the affordances of various objects, or to put it more precisely, in performing this symbolic act, these affordances are acted upon. In order for them to be acted upon, however, they must first be perceived. This can be as simple as seeing others do something, like with the planting of flower bulbs in Groningen and in Alphen aan den Rijn, or just seeing the effects of these earlier actions as with the Herinnerdingen in Apeldoorn and Groningen, but less so in Castricum. For other affordances more guidance was needed, like with the singing of the names or possibly with some of the collective commemorations in Alphen aan den Rijn. Perception is of course strongly related to the degree in which actions, or maybe more properly the objects involved in them, are recursive. The fact that candles afford lighting or that flower bulbs afford planting is readily perceived because these acts have been done before. In other cases, such as the Floating Lights, however, it is the fact that the acting upon some affordances leaves recognisable traces which trigger perception and possibly imitation.

In summary then it could be said that the recursive affordances of material culture used in these examples facilitated the perception of certain performative affordances, that when acted upon led to symbolic interpretations of messages being communicated. Several comments are called for regarding each of these points however. First it has to be pointed out that when the recursive affordances of an object are not, or not yet, sufficiently available, the resulting lack of perception of its relevant affordances can be compensated for by enhancing perception in other ways, such as with the contrast between light and dark discussed above, or of course the presence of people pointing these affordances out. Additionally, it is important to note that only certain affordances of all those that can be acted upon, should also be acted upon in a ritual setting, and it is through this selection of ritually relevant affordances that action can become framed performance. However, perceiving and acting upon the relevant performative affordances does not dictate the symbolic interpretations that people make, a point made before when talking about personal symbolism and the relationality of affordances. As such the lighting of exactly the same type of tea lights had the symbolic affordance of not leaving one's daughter behind in the dark to one person, while they had the affordance of seeing the name of one's father slowly burn out, to another. Besides affordances being relational and thus dependent on the person involved, there are also external factors of influence, such as the wind temporarily not blowing Floating Lights towards the others. The emerging effects of these relational and contextual influences on the types of messages that are being perceived is evident from that same example, with the coming together of the Floating Lights implicitly bringing forth the canonical image of the coming together of the souls, and the lack of this taking place being interpreted as a more self referential message about that particular individual.

Although it will by now be clear that the affordances of objects are of influence on the ritual effects of the Allerzielen Alom celebrations, this does not answer the primary question of what part these affordances play in the ongoing development of Allerzielen Alom, this issue will therefore be more closely investigated in the next chapter.

Chapter Four:

Developing Allerzielen Alom

As mentioned in the introduction, sixteen Allerzielen Alom evenings, or historically related celebrations, are planned for 2009. Four are new celebrations organised by Van der Lee and her Allerzielen Alom foundation, namely those in Graft-De Rijp, Edam, Velsen and Westzaan, two new celebrations are organised by Schatten van Brabant[31] in Waalwijk en Bergen op Zoom, two are new initiatives, namely those in Dordrecht and Vlaardingen, while the other eight are recurring celebrations, either under the Allerzielen Alom name or another, being Amsterdam IJburg, Alphen aan den Rijn, Apeldoorn, Castricum, Leeuwarden, Schagen, Winschoten and of course De Nieuwe Ooster (Van der Lee 2007: Wat-Ontwikkelingen 2005-2009). To find out how the organisers of these celebrations relate to the objects they use, interviews were conducted with those of the celebrations visited in 2008. As these interviews were held in the summer of 2009, and thus in between celebrations, this was taken as an opportunity to reflect back upon the material culture used in 2008, to inquire about the plans for 2009. This also provided the clear focus that is needed in this type of semi-structured interviews. From each of the interviews, one theme that emerged from the conversations about objects and development, has been chosen and is presented below.

4.1 Alphen aan den Rijn: Maintaining the Initiative[32]

When Hedi Hegeman, who studied both art history and theology, first encountered Van der Lee's booklet, she thought that Allerzielen Alom might be a good way of calling new attention to her

---

[31] Meaning: Treasures of Brabant, a foundation of the Province of Noord-Brabant.
[32] The following is based on an interview with Hedi Hegeman on 01-07-09.

own private company for ritual guidance named Kairos Rituelen after having been out of the running due to a brain infarct. The idea was not, however, to have the celebration be a one time thing, and she was therefore very happy that last year's reception was good enough that this year she can not count just on the funerary company that supported her last year, but also on the other ones that work in the town. Despite this positive reception in local newspapers as well as the surveys that were handed out, Hedi is convinced that there is still a lot to be learned from last year's celebration and the survey mentioned in chapter three was a good guideline for that. One of the things coming out of that survey was that the collective explanation at the beginning was not required, and the focus next year will therefore be more on just providing opportunities for collective commemoration. As her main goal is providing options, she does not want too strict a structure, although she does want to give more space, and pay more attention to the placing of each possibility for collective commemoration so that they will more clearly visible. There are no new options for collective commemorations being planned, although due to popular demand in the surveys there is going to be more opportunity for listening to music together as well as for sharing drinks and for talking with each other. She does not think it's a good idea to place more benches or hay bales to sit on, as was also requested, as that would probably make the atmosphere less informal. The lane running from the coffee building to the memorial circle, will also be the main axis again, although several new sections such as the urn garden will also be illuminated. The availability of the coffee building is also important as a safe haven for when it would rain and the normal plans could not go through. Although she would try, in such a case, to stimulate the visitors to at least visit the graves and maybe put up a party tent outside. Despite some reaction, the gate is going to be closed again, to enhance the feeling of togetherness, although she is considering options to include the area outside of the gate into the celebration, maybe by having a choir sing there or asking a local artist to design lights that can float in the pond next to the entrance, nothing interactive though, as that belongs inside. The plan, in any case, is to involve local artist organisations more than the two statues that were displayed last year. These were also not very visible because the artist had not wanted Hedi to illuminate them too strongly. Regarding such differences in opinion Hedi stresses that she as a ritual guide needs to maintain control over things as she has the needed expertise to bring people together to share their experiences. This same point also comes up regarding the funeral companies. Monuta, the company supporting her last year had helped her with acquiring licenses and obtaining the 400 grave candles used to illuminate the paths. With more companies being involved this year, however, she is afraid that limiting their influence to such practical matters might become more difficult. One of the issues that she also wants to guard is the religious neutrality of the location, and she was therefore none to happy that the municipality has given a recurring license for the actual All Souls' Day instead of the requested first Saturday of November. Wanting to protect the continuity of her initiative does not however mean that Hedi is not still looking for better ways of doing and using things, as will be clear from the above, and even more importantly, she points out that not every year can or even should be the same.

4.2 Apeldoorn: Local Adaptation[33]

Like Hedi, Alinde Vrolijk took the initiative to organise an Allerzielen Alom celebration after encountering Van der Lee's booklet. Being a ritual guide and a singing pedagogue herself, she decided to organise the event together with Maria de Greef, a mourning counsellor who then still ran a funeral company, and Mirjam Jansen, owner of a spiritual shop. The cooperation had been smooth and beneficial as each had their own lines of influence, although this year a fourth woman, Grietje Vermeer, a mourning counsellor and social worker, will join them as the work had been a bit too much last year, especially as the goal is to set a trend that can be handed over to others in a couple of years. The Soerenseweg cemetery had been chosen because it's a municipal monument with good accessibility. The municipality also supported the project financially as well as through some manpower. The cemetery itself is also the main source of inspiration for the form of the celebration and just two days before the interview, Alinde and the others had been walking over it to get ideas for this year. As they had already decided to lengthen the celebration with an hour, the route had to be made longer as well. However, the one now created is not the definite one yet, as they will come back to the cemetery in September together with the company that had provided the electric lighting last year, as these men have another way of looking at things, especially now they know what to expect. Walking around they had also decided that unlike last year all the torches will be

---

[33] The following is based on an interview with Alinde Vrolijk on 03-07-09.

put on the left side of the route this year, to enhance clarity. The Stilteplek will not be continued this year, both because the wind kept blowing out the candles and because the concept hadn't really worked. Instead some benches will probably be put up near the new children's monument, maybe in combination with something like a harp being played. Another change to the route was needed to make the location for the singing of the names more visible, especially since this had provided an important emotional experience to the visitors. Alinde has the suspicion that the flowing lines that were present in the cord indicating the place for the planting of the flower bulbs as well as the ribbons that could be hung on a line and the Golf van Herinnering, are reflections of the flowing lines of the cemetery itself, as they had been thought up with this cemetery in mind. Interestingly the primary reason behind the shape chosen for the Golf van Herinnering was that it did not necessitate a carpenter like the original Herinnerdingen would.

As the celebration is still in its early stage, they are only going to introduce two new things this year, one being the benches near the children's monument, while the other, although not completely developed yet, will involve the ancient graves near the entrance to stress the importance of those that came before us. Something that Alinde would have liked to be able to do were the Floating Lights as it would not have been too extreme and would have fitted the setting, the cemetery does not have a pond however. Similarly the Thai Sky Lanterns would have been appropriate but they are made impossible by the abundance of trees on the cemetery. Other forms presented in the booklet, like the paraffin statues or vegetable patches on graves are far too extreme or, like the named laundry, would require too much explanation. Here Alinde stresses that in all of these cases it is important to realise that there is a difference in culture between Amsterdam and Apeldoorn, which is located in a much more strictly Christian part of the country. Due to this fact something like the Hiernamaals might possibly be used, but would then have to be adapted by altering the name into something like 'Characters'. The Golf van Herinnering worked pretty well on that account, as it did not evoke any particular religious imagery. In the future Alinde and the others do want to stimulate people to do more at the graves than just placing some candles as this can trigger interesting conversations between visitors.

On a related point Alinde stresses that they want to work with local artists, even more so because they have to be volunteers or else it is not affordable. Finding funds has also proven to be difficult and they are now looking for local funds, which again makes it important that the forms used fit in with local expectations and tolerances. The municipality did renew their support, which is also to be used for a website on which they want to place their own, locally appropriate, pictures as well as quotes from the Golf van Herinnering and the correspondence cards that could be filled in at the coffee tables.

4.3 Castricum: Community Celebration[34]

After the success of the celebration in 2007, several people in Castricum wanted it to be continued in the following year. Eventually Marina van der Wal, a mourning councillor, became the new organiser together with Raldi Beentjes, a student of social work studies. As will be clear from the description given in chapter three, their version of Allerzielen Alom was different to those organised by Van der Lee on several points. One of these, the decision to illuminate the entire cemetery instead of illuminating only a set route was pointed out by both of them as a conscious effort to include everybody into the celebrations, not just those that happened to lie by one of the main paths. For the coming celebration the desirability of a clearer route is however still a point of discussion between the two of them. In either case it is the focus on including the whole local community that to them is more important than a focus on art, which they consider secondary to the importance of bringing the community together and make it something for the people of Castricum, by the people of Castricum. The goal then is to create a place for yearly commemoration, nothing more. Their task then is to create the framework by illuminating the cemetery, arranging food, drink and some music and the rest is to be filled in by local people who organise something, either at the grave or elsewhere, when needed with their guidance or practical support. They expect that this way it will also be easier to hand the organisation over to others in a year of five, so that the celebration will remain a recurring thing.

By keeping it small and focusing on the community, the financial side of the celebration is now also becoming more self-sustaining. As their combined networks cover most of Castricum it was relatively easy for them to find local companies willing to help for the sake of the community, or in return for some modest advertisement. Last year this approach made it possible to organise

---

[34] The following is based on an interview with Marina van der Wal en Raldi Beentjes 06-07-09.

the celebration without any funding and for the coming celebration they had not even needed to ask around as much anymore as one company offered 250 new torches after having overheard a conversation and the man who had put up the electricity last year hadn't been happy about the electric lighting and had thus made some arrangements for the coming celebration. Similarly the two potted trees that had been contributed by a local horticulturalist did not have to be returned, while the man who maintained the three fire baskets at the urn wall had been annoyed by the mess resulting from the paper messages and had thus made two to three hundred small wooden planks that can be hung in them during the coming celebration instead. The teacher who had created the doors with poetry and the woman handing out the wooden disks had been such individual initiatives as well.

Of course, the majority of individual initiatives concern the things organised by the graves. As said in chapter two, there had already been many such grave decorations and graveside activities in 2007, but when Marina en Raldi took over they found this the most important thing to stress, the rest being the secondary framework. This stressing is partially done in the preparatory meetings where some handles are given, but in most cases people now come up with their own ideas and either develop it privately or ask questions about its feasibility through e-mail or by approaching them in the street. When needed, people are then given some more guidance to make sure that their ideas find an appropriate form. Although the results could be viewed as a move to the individual level, Raldi and Marina stress that the conversations that come out of the decorations and activities at the grave make it a very communal happening, with people learning about the stories behind the graves.

Despite their focus on the community, however, both Raldi and Marina are also working on some contributions to the celebration themselves, although again with the community in mind. Raldi for example has come up with the idea of placing rotating drying racks on the graveyard, probably with poems written by local secondary school students hanging from them, and Marina is working with somebody from Vluchtelingen Werk Nederland[35] on a project involving suitcases filled with personal memories that are going to be placed throughout the cemetery by both fugitives and locals.

---

[35] Vluchtelingen Werk Nederland is a Dutch non-profit organisation that supports fugitives residing in the Netherlands.

4.4 De Nieuwe Ooster: Dealing with Success[36]

The yearly Herinnering Verlicht celebration at De Nieuwe Ooster is primarily organised by Carla van der Elst, the park's communications advisor, together with the heads of the indoor and of the outdoor departments of the company. With them she discusses the artists that she has come across or that presented their services, as well as such things as routings. From there gradually more people get involved, and for these employees the celebration has gone a long way from an initial dislike for artists and their strange practices on their cemetery, to a yearly event that brings not only the employees together, but also brings them into closer contact with the park's community of bereaved. The evaluation afterwards is also an important point of reference for possible improvements as well as new ideas. Many lessons have also been learned from the previous years. In the first year it was expected that there would be many complaints, instead there was only one of a man who had already been in the park during the preparations and he had a feeling of desacralisation. From this they learned that it is important to have the basics secured well beforehand, with everything being tested, and alternative plans for weather dependent concepts having been worked out. These basics, such as the light and fire plan, an endpoint with hot drinks and the small ritual acts, have by now more or less found their form, with all the materials needed for them being in stock and relevant artistic contacts being listed and their role being clearly defined. Carla therefore also speaks of the tradition that has been given shape, although this is also a point for concern, because it can never be clear whether such conditions as financial means remain available in the future. They have also been working, therefore, on a plan that would be feasible with less means.

Not only finances are reasons for change, however, because the precise choices of what is used in any given year is not fixed and thus, while the ritual act of writing messages will for example be recurrent, the actual shape of such a location for collective commemoration is not. Carla stresses that it is probably even a necessity to be continuously searching, otherwise it becomes the mere repetition of the same old song. In this search it is important to keep listening to the visitors. One man, for example, told her in 2008 that it had been a fantastic evening but that there had been so much to do that he spent little time at the grave of his daughter. This ties in to what Carla identifies as the major challenge at the

---

[36] The following is based on an interview with Carla van der Elst on 30-06-09.

moment, namely the celebration's popularity. With 5000 visitors in 2008, Carla is worrying if it is not becoming too big, and the goal for the 2009 celebration therefore is to bring these numbers back to 3500 to 4000 by putting the focus more on the people who actually have somebody to commemorate than commemoration in general. On a material level this means toning down such things as lasers, not putting a banner on the fence and maybe pointing out in communications that people should come to commemorate, not for yet another new spectacle. They are also planning to give people more handles for doing things at the graves themselves, and they are therefore designing something to hand out, which can be used for such graveside activities. The routing will also probably be changed, for example by shortening it or by cutting it in two halves. Certain popular locations for collective commemoration, like the Floating Lights, also need to be reconsidered as they have become too busy. This could for example be done through replacing the plastic cups with something that has to be paid for, although that does not really fit the policy so far, or by streamlining the process of the putting together of the Floating Lights, although that would mean taking away the opportunity to fuzz around with your own light. Another option would be to skip the Floating Lights for one year, as they had done with the Flag Tree. In some cases dealing with the popularity of the celebration, can even be as simple as facilitating the spontaneous acts that emerge from the masses, for example by taken the plants out of the flower tubs so that the candles can be placed more safely in them at the end of the evening.

4.5 Ida van der Lee: Embedding the Concept[37]

As Ida van der Lee has organised many more celebrations than just the one in Groningen, and is going to be organising in other places than Groningen this year, her booklet and the website were chosen as the focal points for the interview instead. Ida herself is very happy with the booklet and its effect, the fact that it contained so many images and guidelines has inspired more people than she had inspected. The upcoming celebration in Vlaardingen had been inspired by the website instead, although they had also wanted to order 50 copies of the booklet. Regrettably Ida had to decline as the publisher had sold out, and the last copies she herself owns are needed for new initiatives and to convince funds or municipalities. Originally Ida had planned this year's celebrations to be the last,

---

[37] The following is based on an interview with Ida van der Lee on 16-07-09.

but now that the phenomenon is spreading and she feels responsible for it, she is not so sure anymore. In any case, the object for this year's celebrations is not to arrive, unpack and build up like a circus company as they did in 2007, but find a way to involve the community to a greater extent. Hereto a whole range of workshops are going to be organised this year. In addition there are also two two-day master classes for artists that want to participate in Allerzielen Alom, where they are given the relevant information, do some exercises like the Herinnerdingen and are presented with concrete possibilities which Ida took from her meetings with the location managers. In one location, for example, they had the plan to use the named laundry, but as this had been used several times already, Ida is going to hand it over to one of the artists to think of a new form for that concept. Similarly Ida will try to find a graphic designer to work with a lady from Westzaan, who had the idea to place lines of poetry on a path. For most artists, however, these types of collaborations do not come naturally, and the master classes are also meant to select those that are capable of dealing with this loss of autonomy.

Besides these master classes that are meant to bridge the gap between artists and the community, there will also be workshops for amateur artists from the community that have an idea that they want to work out, people interested in fire and light design who are shown the importance of combining the practical aspect with the more artistic aspect of form, meaning and effect as well as a workshop for people who want to be guides or hosts. In one workshop with Daphne Questro an attempt will be made to teach the methods used in the singing of the names and in another a brainstorm will be held with choirs to see how they can adapt their presentation to Allerzielen Alom. For the visitors who want to do something by the graves, workshops will be held for decorating the graves for which two graves in Graft-De Rijp will serve as examples, in addition to pictures made by one artist with the use of an old door and an idea list. As a more accessible option, a workshop will be given in which photographs are made into things like simple lanterns with the use of semi-transparent paper.

Finally a workshop about planning and the making of an action plan will be given to the organisers of the various celebrations, although Ida does not know how many will actually come as the organisers of the recurring celebrations each have their own ideas. Here she notices a certain fear of art and artists in some of the organisers such as those in Winschoten, who wanted to keep things simpler and are now continuing under their own name. The art world partially owes this fear to itself though, as it often has difficulty in being supportive instead of autonomous. As such artists are often sees as troublesome and expensive and people easily think they can design the things themselves. Artists, however, are more sensitive to the workings of form, imagination and meaning and can spend many hours contemplating the best form of which the effect is much stronger even though the hours that went into it are largely invisible. Keeping these forms elegant, functional and without too many distracting fringes is important to create that effect, according to Ida. This way the gap left behind by the falling away of organised religion can be filled in by artists that create forms with meaning that can activate people's imaginations. There is a difficult tension there, where a balance has to be found between the importance of repetition for ritual acts and the necessity of keeping the form sharp and up to date, like with the named laundry. Sometimes these forms can become to confrontational, as with the paraffin statues for which Ida had to convince the artist to place them upright as the lying down position had to strong an association with corpses. The example of the Herinnerdingen shows, however, that sometimes a new more effective form can simply come out of a problem with finding people willing to participate, while the presence of empty compartments in the columbarium in Groningen led to yet another new form.

4.6 Discussion and Analysis

Summarising the above, it is interesting to see that for each stage of the development of Allerzielen Alom there are different themes that surfaced when discussing the use of material culture. In Alphen aan den Rijn an important concern is in finding partners to work with, without giving them control over the form of the celebration, while in Apeldoorn the main issue is in finding material forms that fit in with the local culture. In Castricum, where this local aspect has moulded the original concept into a somewhat different shape, the organisers are now loosening the controls on material culture towards the community. At De Nieuwe Ooster, where the various roles of those involved have been defined for several years now, they are now confronted with the need to adapt the shape of the celebration to account for, or even curb, its popularity. Finally, for Ida and her foundation, the main challenge is in setting up new celebrations in such a way that a lasting bridge is struck between local participation and the special expertise provided by artists. No matter what issues surfaced, however, it came up in relation to how the organiser's were dealing with material culture. More importantly, the solution for these issues are also sought after in relation to those objects. As such, objects can be seen as an important interface between the concepts, goals, experiences, people and other factors involved. But as any medium, material culture, with its myriad affordances, is far from neutral. And as these affordances are emergent, relational and not fully transparent there will always be differences between intent and outcome. This, combined with the desire for rites to be effective, might be behind the need for continuous search for better forms and shapes that was expressed in each of the interviews.

Conclusion

Going back to the main question posed in the introduction, the answer would be that material culture is indeed of influence, not only on the ritual effects of the Allerzielen Alom celebrations, but also on the way the organisers are developing them. And they do so by being an interface between the various goals set forward by the organisers, and the experiences of the visitors. The reason they can function as such an interface is because organisers can present the objects in such a way that their recursive affordances facilitate the perception of certain performative affordances, that when acted upon afford symbolic interpretations of messages being communicated. Trying to influencing an object's affordances in such a way is, however, far from straightforward as they are emergent, relational and not fully transparent, and as such there will always be differences between intent and outcome, necessitating constant adaptation.

By doing so, however, the actions undertaken by the visitors can come to feel natural, as if they are reacting while they are actually creating, which makes the actions more effective. In lieu of dogmatic traditions or myths supporting Allerzielen Alom, this focus on a ritual action having to be effective was mentioned in chapter one as characteristic of present-day ritualising. Looking closer at the ritual affordances of material culture, it turns out to be only logical that material culture is therefore important in implicitly religious actions. Because, without having to go into explicit and dogmatic justifications of apparent contradictions, material culture can greatly enhance the effective ambiguity that was said to be so important in staving of ontological insecurity. Through their recursive and performative affordances, actions can be made to seem the natural way of doing things by framing them so that a temporary ritual world can come to pass, without actually having to leave the real world. And through their symbolic and communicative affordances a link can be made between personal and communal interpretations while simultaneously connecting the immanent meaning of the current situation to canonical or transcendent meanings. This way, through the interface of material culture, religious ideas, community and tradition can find a place in a world that is said to be secularising, individualising and losing touch with its past. Thus it might even be said that due to the absence of any explicit or dogmatic justifications for ritual action, dealing with the ritual affordances of material culture has become an inescapable aspect of implicitly religious contemporary ritualizing.

This also means that studies of present-day emerging rites would lose sight of a fundamental aspect of their topic, when they would ignore the role of objects. Even for Allerzielen Alom, research into the influence of material culture is far from exhausted, as the relation between visitors and objects has only been touched upon in passing. In any case, future research into this topic is important to challenge, and thus further develop, both the methods and the conclusions of the exploratory investigation that was presented here.

References

Arfman, William R.
2008 *Visiting the Calvarion at Mitla, Oaxaca, a critical look at the continuity of a religious practice.* Sidestone Press, Leiden.

Armstrong, Robert Plant
1971 *The Affecting Presence: An Essay in Humanistic Anthropology.* University of Illinois Press, Urbana.

Bailey, Edward I.
1997 *Implicit Religion in Contemporary Society.* Kok Pharos Publishing House, Kampen.

Bell, Catherine
1997 *Ritual, Perspectives and Dimensions.* Oxford University Press, Oxford.

Bolt, Sophie, Meike Heesels and Eric Venbrux
2008 Rituele creativiteit rondom de dood. In: *Rituele Creativiteit, Actuele veranderingen in de uitvaart en rouwcultuur in Nederland.* Eds. Eric Venbrux, Meike Heesels and Sophie Bolt. Meinema, Zoetermeer.

Dant, Tim
1999 *Material Culture in the Social World.* Open University Press, Buckingham.
2005 *Materiality and Society.* Open University Press, Maidenhead.

De Maaker, Erik, Eric Venbrux and Stijn Westrik
2008 Een nieuw bestaan voor de doden. In: *Allerzielen Alom, Kunst tot Herdenken.* Meinema, Zoetermeer, pp 59-70.

De Maaker, E., T. Quartier, J. Wojtkowiak and E. Venbrux
2008 Kreatives Totengedenken: Rituelle Erinnerungsräume in einem niederländischen Kunstprojekt. In: Jaarboek voor liturgieonderzoek 24, 155-176.

Gibson, James J.
1979 *The Ecological Approach to Visual Perception.* Houghton Miflin Company, Boston.

Graves-Brown, Paul M.
2000   Introduction. In: *Matter, Materiality and Modern Culture*. Ed. Paul M. Graves-Brown. Routledge, London.

Grimes, Ronald, L.
2000   *Deeply into the Bone: re-inventing rites of passage*. University of California Press, London.

Houseman, Michael
2008   Relationality. In: *Theorizing Rituals. Classical Topics, Theoretical Approaches, Analytical Concepts*. Eds. Jens Kreinath, Jan Snoek and Michael Stausberg. Brill, Leiden. 413-428.

Knappett, Carl
2005   The Affordances of Things: a Post-Gibsonian Perspective on the Relationality of Mind and Matter. In: *Rethinking Materiality: The Engagement of Mind with the Material World*. Eds: E.DeMarrais, C.Gosden & C.Renfrew. McDonald Institute for Archaeological Research, Cambridge, p.p.43-52.

Kopytoff, Igor
1986   *The cultural biography of things: commoditization as process*. In: *The Social Life of Things: Commodities in cultural perspective*, 64-91. Cambridge University Press, Cambridge.

Langer, R., D. Lüddeckens, K. Radde and J. Snoek
2006   Transfer of Ritual. In: *Journal of Ritual Studies* 20 (1), pp.1-10.

Maaker, Erik de, Stijn Westrik and Eric Venbrux
2008   Een nieuw bestaan voor de doden. In: *Allerzielen Alom, Kunst tot Herdenken*. Meinema, Zoetermeer, pp 59-70.

Malafouris, Lambros
2005   The Cognitive Basis of Material Engagement: Where Brain, Body and Culture Conflate. In: *Rethinking Materiality: The Engagement of Mind with the Material World*. Eds: E.DeMarrais, C.Gosden & C.Renfrew. McDonald Institute for Archaeological Research, Cambridge, p.p.53-62.

McDannell, Colleen
1995   *Material Christianity*. Yale University Press, London.

REFERENCES

Quartier, Thomas
2009 *Rouwrituelen: een rituele slinger.* Lezing tijdens het symposium 'Veranderende rituelen rond de dood' van de Radboud Universiteit Webdocument: http://www.ru.nl/soeterbeeckprogramma/terugblik retrieved on 10-07-09.

Quartier, T., E. Venbrux, S. Westrik and J. Wojkowiak
2008 Profiel, ervaringen en religieuze denkbeelden van bezoekers. In: *Allerzielen Alom, Kunst tot Herdenken.* Meinema, Zoetermeer, pp 37-48.

Rappaport, Roy
1999 *Ritual and Religion in the making of humanity.* Cambridge University Press, Cambridge.

Renfrew, Colin
2005 Towards a Theory of Ritual Engagement. In: *Rethinking Materiality: The Engagement of Mind with the Material World.* Eds: E.DeMarrais, C.Gosden & C.Renfrew. McDonald Institute for Archaeological Research, Cambridge, p.p.23-32.

Smith, Jonathan Z.
2004 Religion, Religions, Religious. In: *Relating Religion. Essays in the Study of Religion,* Chicago, 215-229.

Ter Borg, Meerten
2008 Non-institutional Religion in Modern Society. In: *Implicit Religion.* Vol. 11(2), 127-139.

Van der Lee, Ida
2007 *Allerzielen Alom.* Webdocument: http://www.allerzielenalom.nl/index2.html. Retrieved 12-07-2009.
2008 De doden niet verzwijgen maar vieren om wie ze waren en wat ze te vertellen hebben. In: *Allerzielen Alom, Kunst tot Herdenken.* Meinema, Zoetermeer.

Woodward, Ian
2007 *Understanding Material Culture.* Sage Publications, London.